POPE FRANCIS'
REVOLUTION OF TENDERNESS AND LOVE

POPE FRANCIS' REVOLUTION OF TENDERNESS AND LOVE

Theological and Pastoral Perspectives

WALTER KASPER
Translated by William Madges

Paulist Press
New York / Mahwah, NJ

Jacket design by Trace Murphy
Book design by Lynn Else
Front jacket photo courtesy of L'Osservatore Romano
Author jacket photo, back flap, courtesy of the Kardinal Walter Kasper Institut für Theologie, Ökumene und Spiritualität

Library of Congress Control Number: 2015933313

ISBN 978-0-8091-0623-3 (hardcover)
ISBN 978-1-58768-545-3 (e-book)

Published by Paulist Press
997 Macarthur Boulevard
Mahwah, New Jersey 07430

www.paulistpress.com

Printed and bound in the
United States of America

Contents

PREFACE

The present book came into being as a result of fleshing out lectures that I gave at the Catholic Academy of Bavaria in Munich, at the University of Vienna, and at the Theological College of St. George in Frankfurt am Main, as well as in English at the Center for Union in Rome and the Catholic University of America in Washington, DC. I would also like to express here my sincere thanks to the Catholic University of America for the honor of receiving the Johannes Quasten Award.

The book will be published on the occasion of the second anniversary of the pontificate of Pope Francis. Therefore, the manuscript had to be completed in the first week of December 2014. Later publications, speeches, and events could no longer be considered for inclusion.

To Paulist Press and especially to Fr. Mark-David Janus I express my thanks for the excellent editing and publishing support; my thanks as well to Prof. William Madges for the outstanding translation.

Wangen im Allgäu, on the feast of the Epiphany, 2015

Walter Kasper

List of Abbreviations

TEXTS FROM THE
SECOND VATICAN COUNCIL

AA. *Apostolicam actuositatem*. Decree on the Apostolate of the Laity

AG. *Ad gentes*. Decree on the Church's Missionary Activity

CD. *Christus Dominus*. Decree on the Bishops' Pastoral Office in the Church

DV. *Dei Verbum*. Dogmatic Constitution on Divine Revelation

GS. *Gaudium et spes*. Pastoral Constitution on the Church in the Modern World

LG. *Lumen gentium*. Dogmatic Constitution on the Church

NA. *Nostra Aetate*. Declaration on the Relationship of the Church to Non-Christian Religions

UR. *Unitatis Redintegratio*. Decree on Ecumenism

OTHER TEXTS OF THE
CHURCH'S MAGISTERIUM

DH. Heinrich Denzinger, *Enchiridion symbolorum definitionum et declarationum de rebus fidei et morum*, ed. Peter Hünermann, 44th ed. (Freiburg i. Br.: Herder, 2014)

EG. *Evangelii gaudium*. (Joy of the Gospel) Apostolic Exhortation of Pope Francis on the Proclamation of the Gospel in Today's World (2013)

EN. *Evangelii nuntiandi*. Apostolic Exhortation of Pope Paul VI on Evangelization in the Modern World (1975)

I

POPE OF SURPRISES

The election of Cardinal Jorge Mario Bergoglio as bishop of Rome and thereby as universal shepherd of the Catholic Church was a surprise. Already surprising, indeed like a bolt of lightning out of a clear blue sky, was the announcement of the resignation of Pope Benedict XVI on February 11, 2013. Up to that point in time, hardly anyone had imagined such an event. But soon enough the initial speechlessness that most Catholic (and also many non-Catholic) Christians felt—even the bewilderment of many—made room for the insight that this resignation was a courageous, noble, and humble act deserving deep respect.[1] By taking this step, the papacy was not damaged, as many feared; rather, it had become more human and especially more spiritual. By this act, the door was opened to a new epoch in the history of the papacy, which is not bereft of changes. For the resignation of a pope was already envisaged as a possibility in canon law. But now for the first time in the modern history of the church, a reality had developed out of this possibility. A new situation, which had never existed before in this form, took the stage.

The new situation hit the Catholic Church and the Roman Curia at a critical moment. The *Vatileaks*, the published documents stolen from the pope's desk, and suspicions concerning irregularities in financial conduct, especially with regard to the so-called Vatican Bank (Institute for the Works of Religion), showed that many things no longer functioned in the Curia as one was accustomed and could expect to be the case.[2] The crisis, however, reached deeper than the signs of crisis in the Roman Curia. The cases of abuse had unleashed a shock wave and caused serious damage, above all in the United States, Ireland, Belgium, and Germany. Additionally, there arose the impression of mental fatigue and exhaustion, a lack of confidence and enthusiasm. The church was increasingly occupied primarily with itself; it suffered and moaned about its situation or occasionally celebrated itself. Its prophetic power appeared extinguished and its missionary vitality appeared to languish. A world that had become secular and that was no longer communist, but rather consumerist and determined by the economy, appeared to make the church marginal. Booming Pentecostal churches and esotericism throughout the world threatened to outstrip it. A relentless downward spiral appeared to be in motion.[3]

So, the conclave after the resignation of Pope Benedict stood under a completely different portent than the conclave eight years previously. Then, after the more than quarter-century-long pontificate of Pope John Paul II, the church publicly appeared to be in good shape. Heads of state from the entire world and, for the first time in the history of the church, the highest representatives of the non-Catholic churches bowed at the funeral ceremony before this great figure, who had decisively influenced the postwar history of Europe and the world and who had given the Catholic Church its face. For that reason, continuity more than anything else was expected in the election of his successor. Cardinal Joseph Ratzinger, because of his long-standing collaboration with Pope John Paul II, was deemed to be, both theologically and spiritually, the dependable guarantor for this continuity. With the choice of the name *Benedict*, the patron saint of Europe, he expressed his rootedness in the best European tradition. On this basis, he has bequeathed a pure, spiritual legacy that will continue to be cherished into the future.

The resignation of Benedict XVI revealed to everyone overnight and in blatant fashion the concealed crisis that was already present eight years ago. The helmsman on board, on account of the rapid decline of his physical strength, saw that he was no longer able to keep a firm hand on the tiller of the bark of Peter in the stormy waters of a rapidly changing world. The answer to the question of who would be capable of taking the helm, and what the church's course could be in this difficult situation while keeping the necessary consensus of the church, was admittedly anything but clear.

In this situation it was natural that the attention of many was directed away from the tired-looking churches of Europe to the young churches in the South. There too there are many problems, but contrary to old Europe, where secularization is making rapid advances, there is still much Christian substance. While at the beginning of the twentieth century only about a quarter of Catholics lived outside of Europe, at the end of the century less than a quarter lived in Europe. In the course of one century, the Catholic Church had turned itself upside down demographically. Since the Second Vatican Council (1962–1965), it has become a world church, in a new, even sociologically identifiable way; and the church sees itself confronted, in all local churches in different and partially delayed ways, with a rapid cultural and social transformation.

During the informal conversations among the cardinals during the period before the conclave, and during the congregations of cardinals that took place every day during the vacancy of the papacy, different names were mentioned, but no name was singled out to whom the election could fall. The name of the archbishop of Buenos Aires, Cardinal Jorge Mario Bergoglio, was not on the list of *papabili* that journalists were accustomed to put together before the election of a new pope. Admittedly, he was known to insiders since the previous conclave of 2005, when his name was already in discussion. But the fact that he was now seventy-seven years old, not in too robust of health, and was about to go into retirement—and additionally that he was a non-European from the other end of the world and a member of the Jesuit order, from which no pope had arisen heretofore—made his election rather improbable for most observers.

In the period before the conclave, Cardinal Jorge Mario Bergoglio, in an impressive intervention, put his finger clearly on the weak spots of an inward-looking church that no longer radiates its mission. His plea for a church that takes its missionary work to the peripheries made a strong impression.[4] However, that didn't decide anything. According to the way things stood, the decision could be reached only in the conclave, and everyone wanted to trust in the assistance of God's Spirit for that decision.[5]

So it was in no way clearly predictable, but rather a surprise that Cardinal Bergoglio, already on the evening of the second day of the conclave, could receive more than two-thirds of the votes of the eligible cardinals, and was thereby elected on March 13, 2013 as the 265th successor of the Apostle Peter. Not a few cardinals subsequently expressed their impression that "something" moved in this conclave. It was not some kind of wheeling and dealing or clever powers of persuasion. It was palpable, as the pope subsequently expressed it at his reception for the cardinals, "It is Christ who leads the church by means of his Spirit."[6]

Immediately after his election, the pope of surprises arranged for a further surprise by his choice of name. No pope had previously chosen the name *Francis*. It quickly became clear that this was more than the choice of a name; the name was a program for action. At his first meeting with the representatives of the media, the new pope explained his choice of name with a reference to Francis of Assisi: "He is a man of poverty, a man of peace, a man who loves and safeguards creation." And the pope added, "Oh, how I would like a poor church for the poor!"[7] With those words, as would soon become evident, the important motto of the new pontificate was announced. Pope Francis turned those words immediately into deed by eschewing the traditional signs of papal pomp and privilege during his first appearance in the loggia of St. Peter's. He appeared in a plain white cassock with his metal cross that he had already worn as bishop. No liturgical greeting followed, but a simple greeting, completely devoid of melodrama: "Buona sera!"

Surprisingly, he spoke of himself not as *pope* but as *bishop of Rome*. In this way he was reaching back to the earliest tradition. To be the bishop of the Church of Rome, which Ignatius of Antioch already around the middle of the second century described as the church that presides over others in a union of love, was and is no mere afterthought, but it is the basis of the universal pastoral office of the pope.[8] With this self-characterization, especially with an eye to the churches of the East, Pope Francis gave a clear, ecumenical sign that was reason enough for the Ecumenical Patriarch Bartholomew to participate in the official installation of the pope on March 19. When at the end, right before granting his apostolic blessing, the new pope asked the people present to pray that God might bless him and then bowed deeply, a reverent silence that lasted several minutes immediately came over the jam-packed St. Peter's Square. Everyone could sense that something new was dawning with this pope. "And now, we take up this journey—bishop and people—the journey of the Church of Rome, which presides in charity over all the churches."[9]

The word *way*—a fundamental word in the Bible for God's journey with his people; Jesus himself said that he is the way (John

14:6), and the first Christians understood themselves as people of the New Way (Acts 19:9, 23)—was a favorite word already of Cardinal Bergoglio and now is a further key word for the new style of this pontificate. In conversations with his friend, Rabbi Abraham Skorka, he said, "In my personal experience with God I cannot do without the path. I would say that one encounters God walking, moving, seeking him and allowing oneself to be sought by him….That can happen on different paths, the path of pain, of joy, of light, of darkness."[10] In a speech during his visit to an evangelical community in Caserta (see chapter 8, "Ecumenical Vision," below), the pope adds in his characteristic manner, "Christians who stand still: that does no good, for what stands still, what does not move, goes bad like standing water. The water that goes bad first of all is the water that does not flow."[11]

The question therefore was, What will be the path of the new pope, together with the people of God? Of course, it will be the path or way of discipleship of Jesus Christ. There is no other path for the church. But that was and is clearly a path full of surprises. Not the least of surprises was that the pope succeeded in short order to brighten up the pessimistic mood, which had rested upon the church like a blight because of stagnation, scandals, and the problems that became public because of the *Vatileaks*. Surprisingly, Pope Francis has breathed new life into the church, the breath of confidence, of joy, and of freedom. Surprising and in no way self-evident finally was the altogether favorable attention that the new pope found in the media and in milieus that otherwise preferred to keep their distance from the church.

So it is not surprising that, already one and a half years after his inauguration, so many publications about Pope Francis have appeared that they can scarcely be counted anymore. Most of the publications reflect the high level of acceptance that the pope has found after only a few days and weeks among the overwhelming majority of the people of God and beyond.[12] Of course, critical voices are not absent. They say, We don't like this pope because he pleases too much.[13] In the meantime, the reservations, the open as well as the oblique criticisms in many media and websites, even in many church circles, have increased. That is not surprising. Rather, in light of Jesus' way and the journey of the church in history, the opposite would be surprising. Finally there are not a few who mistrust the new excitement, who exercise lordly temporizing restraint and who more or less want to wait out the papacy in light of the advanced age of the pope. What appears to the vast majority to be a new spring is for them a temporary cold spell, not a new beginning but an intermezzo.

In what follows, we are not dealing with such church-political assessments, biographical details, anecdotes and stories, and much less with gossip about the private details that are playing out, really or allegedly, behind the walls of the Vatican. All of that may be interesting, but it does not touch the heart of the matter. In the following, the attempt will be made to approach the Francis phenomenon theologically and to illuminate somewhat the theological background and the theological substance of his pontificate, and to make clear the new perspectives that are emerging. The positive as well as the critical assessments are in danger of trivializing or treating the pontificate in a banal manner. If some turn the pope into a kind of rock star, so others regard him as a theological lightweight. Pope Francis is neither the one nor the other. Then what?

In order to answer this question to the extent that I am able, I would first like to pursue his theological and spiritual roots and highlight the great tradition in which his pontificate stands. The surprisingly new features of this "pope of surprises"[14] are not some innovations, but rather the eternal newness of the gospel, which is always the same and yet, over and over again, is surprisingly new and always relevant in a new way. Jesus Christ—"his riches and beauty are inexhaustible. He is forever young and a constant source of newness" (*EG* 11). Remembering the gospel and its eternal newness admittedly is also always a dangerous remembering. It raises questions and calls for conversion and a new orientation. Time and again we must allow ourselves to be surprised by God and to break anew out of what is usual. That elicits resistance. That was already the case with Jesus and also the case in the previous history of the church. It cannot be any different today. If it were different, it would certainly not be the gospel of Jesus Christ.

II

CONTINUITY AND REFORM— NOT THE ASHES BUT THE EMBERS

In the attempt to approach the matter theologically, from the very beginning one must guard against two prejudgments, both of which attempt to co-opt Pope Francis in diametrically opposed ways. Some seek to claim him for their own ideas of reform, especially for the reform ideas that are well known in the Western world, and to measure him according to whether or, as the case may be, the extent to which he meets these expectations. With such expectations, which are bound up with Western discussions of modernization, one cannot do justice to the pope, who comes from the Southern Hemisphere. He doesn't fit into our schema of progressive or conservative, which in the meantime has become somewhat worn-out and outdated. He has clearly distinguished himself from both positions in an impressive closing speech at the extraordinary synod of bishops on October 18, 2014.

The other prejudgment goes in the opposite direction. It sees the obvious differences in personality and style between Francis and Benedict XVI, but immediately adds solicitously that there is not the slightest difference between them in this matter. What is correct is that both popes are Catholic and both champion Catholic teaching. In fact, it will become apparent in what follows that Pope Benedict, with regard to many questions, theologically prepared the present pontificate to a greater extent than may appear at first glance.[1] Pope Francis himself does not skip any opportunity to emphasize this agreement. This continuity is most clearly expressed by the fact that Pope Francis, with only two short additions adopted as his own the encyclical *Lumen fidei* (2013), which had been prepared by Pope Benedict. One cannot express the continuity more clearly than that. Shortly afterward, however, Pope Francis laid out his own program in the Apostolic Exhortation *Evangelii gaudium* (2013). It is a program for the century in which differences are evident—differences not in the truths of faith, but certainly in style, in methodological starting point, and in emphases.

If one wanted to sketch the difference briefly, perhaps also in a somewhat abridged fashion, one could say that Pope Benedict prominently represents, according to background and education, the best European tradition. He proceeds from the faith of the church, seeks to make it accessible and understandable both intellectually and spiritually in order to implement doctrine in practice—corresponding to the traditional determination of the relationship of theory and practice. His manner of speaking consists in instruction that has been spiritually thought through and lived out. Pope Francis, on the other hand, is defined by kerygmatic theology.[2] In this way he is not a covert Franciscan; he is a Jesuit through and through. In the spirit of the founder of his order, Ignatius of Loyola (1491–1556), he proceeds not from doctrine, but from the concrete situation. Naturally, he does not simply intend to accommodate himself to the situation; rather, as is envisaged in the *Spiritual Exercises* of Ignatius, he attempts to evaluate the situation according to the rule for discernment of spirits.

With the help of such spiritual discernment, he then comes to concrete, practical decisions (*EG* 50–51).[3]

The discernment of spirits is talked about already in the New Testament (Rom 12:2; 1 Cor 12:10; 1 Thess 5:21; 1 John 4:1) and then in the entire spiritual tradition. According to Ignatius of Loyola's understanding, discernment wants to give an answer to the question, What does God want of me in this concrete situation? In this sense, Karl Rahner (1904–1984) spoke of an existential knowledge, that is, of the knowledge of the concrete will of God that is directed to the individual for the given situation.[4] As Pope Francis expresses it, we are talking about a completely personal insight: "I am a mission on this earth; that is the reason why I am here in this world" (*EG* 273).

The Second Vatican Council, following Pope John XXIII, applied this method to the church in the pastoral constitution *Gaudium et spes*. The Council sought to proceed from the "signs of the times" and to interpret them in the light of the gospel.[5] Starting with the "signs of the times" caused debate already during the Council. German bishops and theologians, even including the then *peritus* Joseph Ratzinger, would gladly have preferred Christology as the starting point. The question about the relation of doctrine and the concrete situation could not be fully thrashed out during the Council. In the final version of the document, nevertheless, a balance was struck, which then found broad approval.[6]

The theology of liberation took up the methodological change in perspective or shift in paradigm that had been carried out in the pastoral constitution *Gaudium et spes*, in the sense of the three steps of seeing, judging, and acting.[7] This method was developed by the founder of the Catholic Worker Youth (JOC) and later Cardinal Joseph Cardijn (1882–1967) and was explicitly recommended by Pope John XXIII in his social encyclical *Mater et magistra* (1961).[8] The general assemblies of the Latin American episcopate (CELAM) have embraced this method in Medellin (1968), Puebla (1979), and then again in Aparecida (2007).[9] In Aparecida Cardinal Jorge Bergoglio was the chair of the editorial committee and, as such, was the architect of the document that was decided on by this gathering, which then as pope he described as the key to understanding the mission of the church in his speech to the bishops of Brazil on the occasion of World Youth Day 2013 in Rio de Janeiro.

The difference between Pope Benedict and Pope Francis thus goes back far, but it does not concern theological truth. Rather, it concerns theological method and its concomitant emphases, as well as Pope Francis' style, which is less didactic and more kerygmatic. With reference to the older as well as the more recent history of the papacy, such differences are nothing new, but rather are an expression of Catholic unity in diversity, as well as a sign of a not defunct but living tradition that is guided by God's Spirit. The entire history of the papacy is full of such unity in diversity and difference.

One can best clarify in a summary fashion the question of continuity and discontinuity with the help of the famous speech that Pope Benedict gave to the college of cardinals and the Roman Curia on December 22, 2005. In it Pope Benedict, in reference to the Second Vatican Council, spoke of a hermeneutics of continuity, which he differentiated from a hermeneutics of rupture. But following the great pioneer of modern Catholic theology, John Henry Newman (1801–1890), he distinguished the continuity of principles from discontinuity in practical application and reform.[10] Thus Pope Benedict could describe the hermeneutics of continuity as a hermeneutics of reform.

Pope Francis avowedly wants reforms in the church (EG 26). In the process, he is not a revolutionary in the sense of a subversive, even if many media present him this way and many

Catholics fear so. He is a conservative, but a conservative who, just like John XXIII and the subsequent popes down to Benedict XVI, knows that one can only preserve the heritage of tradition if one does not regard it like a dead coin that is passed on from hand to hand until, in the end, it is totally worn, or does not treat it like a beautiful museum piece stored in a glass case. One can only preserve the tradition by making it present in the power of the Holy Spirit, who is present in the church and who guides it into all truth (John 16:13). Tradition is the content of the apostolic inheritance that is binding for all times, as well as realized ever anew in the Holy Spirit. In this sense, tradition is understood by the Second Vatican Council as a living tradition, in which, with the aid of the Holy Spirit, there is progress and growth in the understanding of the apostolic faith that has been handed on once and for all (*DV* 8; cf. *DH* 3020).

To Thomas More (1478–1535) as well as to John XXIII (1881–1963), this saying has been ascribed: What pertains is not to pass on the ashes, but rather the glowing embers hidden underneath. Pope Francis wants to clear away many of the accumulated ashes in order to bring to light anew the fiery nucleus of the gospel. If one wants to speak of a revolution, then it is not a revolution in the sense of a violent overthrow, but rather, as Francis says, the fervent revolution of tender love, upon whose transforming power from within he relies (*EG* 88; 288).

III

A HISTORICAL-THEOLOGICAL CLASSIFICATION—ARGENTINE AND EUROPEAN ROOTS

Every pope comes out of a certain historical and cultural tradition. Pope Francis is the first pope who hails from a megalopolis of the Southern Hemisphere. Such megalopolises, not only with regard to size but also with regard to the diversity of the ancestry and culture of their populations, are hardly to be compared with one of our big European cities. Buenos Aires, where Jorge Bergoglio grew up and where he later worked as bishop, is, on the one hand, defined by European culture and, at the beginning of the nineteenth century, was regarded as the Paris of Latin America. In addition, there is the typically Argentine culture of the original inhabitants, the gauchos, romanticized in folklore in the nineteenth century, as well as the culture of different immigrants, primarily Italian. Finally, mention must be made of the bleak peripheries and the slums of the poor (*casas miserias*).[1] The evangelization of these pluralistic urban cultures, and especially those on the periphery, was a challenge and a pressing concern for Archbishop Jorge Bergoglio.[2]

Only from the perspective of this background can one understand the theology that has shaped Pope Francis. His most important theology teacher was Lucio Gera (1924–2012). How very much Archbishop Bergoglio held him in esteem emerges from the solitary fact that, after his death in 2012, Archbishop Bergoglio allowed him to be interred in the episcopal crypt of the Buenos Aires cathedral in order to honor him as the father of Argentine theology. Lucio Gera, together with Gustavo Gutierrez, who is regarded as the father of liberation theology, and others took part in the conference in Petropolis in 1964 that had been convened by the Latin American Episcopal Conference (CELAM). It is regarded as the hour in which liberation theology was born. At this conference, Lucio Gera gave a paper on the theme, "The Meaning of the Christian Message in the Context of Poverty and Oppression." This theme has become foundational for all forms of liberation theology. They all operate according to the method of see, judge, act.[3]

The Argentine type of liberation theology, through the decisive influence of Lucio Gera, has nevertheless followed its own path and developed its own profile.[4] Different from other forms that are generally better known to us, Argentine liberation theology does not proceed from an analysis of sociopolitical and economic relations or from antagonisms in society in order then to interpret them with Marxist categories, in the sense of a theory of dependence.[5] Rather, it proceeds from a historical analysis of the culture of the people, who are united by a common ethos. It is a theology of the people and of culture.

In doing so, it does not want to lecture the people, but rather it wants to listen to the people's wisdom. Therefore, a higher value is assigned to popular piety. Naturally, this theology of the people does not overlook the existing social antitheses, but it is not guided by the idea of class warfare, but by the thought of harmony, peace, and reconciliation. This concern shines forth again and again in Pope Francis' responses to conflict situations, as for instance at the impressive vigil for peace in the Middle East on September 7, 2013 in St. Peter's Square, when he spoke of the world as God's creation, as the house of harmony and peace, in which everyone finds his or her place and can feel at home.

This understanding of the people corresponds to the spirit of democratic romanticism that found its way into Argentina at the end of the nineteenth century and superseded the previous politics of culture, which was in the mode of the European Enlightenment. That happened under the influence of the philosophy of the German thinker Karl Christian Friedrich Krause (1781–1832), whose reception in Romance-language countries brought the ideas of Romanticism and German Idealism to Spain and Latin America. People there spoke of "Krausismo." This direction found expression in the Argentine national epic *Martín Fierro* (1872). Pope Francis refers to it explicitly.[6] The epic poem describes the life of a gaucho who, after a long journey, in the end finds the wisdom of a world of justice and community spirit, a world that grants to even the least their dignity and possibilities for personal development.

The populist Peronist movement, which since the 1940s has determined Argentine politics for a long time, did not bring forth for the first time these ideas of a corporate understanding of the people, but rather found them at hand and took hold of them, but then gave them a nationalistic and ideological overlay. Pope Pius XII excommunicated Juan Perón (1895–1974) in 1955; eight years later the excommunication was lifted. Therefore it is too simplistic if one hastily ascribes the Argentine theology of the people to Peronism and, in the process, overlooks its much older roots.[7]

The reference to the influence of the enlightened as well as Romantic-Idealistic European body of thought shows that, despite all of its individuality and originality, Argentine theology—like Argentine culture—has generally strong European roots. Contemporary Argentine theologians are often very familiar with French theology (Henri de Lubac and Yves Congar, among others) and with modern French philosophy (Paul Ricoeur, Emmanuel Levinas, and Jean-Luc Marion, among others). Many of them have studied in Bonn, Innsbruck, Munich, Freiburg, and Tübingen.

Lucio Gera earned his doctorate in Bonn with a classical, Scholastic topic, *The Development of the Doctrine of Transubstantiation from Thomas to Duns Scotus*, and later worked closely with Karl Rahner. In Bonn, thanks to Arnold Rademacher, who earned his doctorate in Tübingen in 1900, Gera became familiar with the ecclesiology of the Tübingen School of the nineteenth century, especially with Johann Adam Möhler (1796–1831) and his teaching about the spirit of the people. The parallels between this Romantic teaching of the early Tübingen theologians about the national spirit, which goes back to Johann Gottfried Herder (1744–1803), and the Argentine theology of the people are striking and clearly not accidental.[8] The relation just shown makes clear how the Argentine form of liberation theology is to be classified in the international context of Catholic theology and in the universal, ecclesial context.

The decisive universal, ecclesial impetus emanated from the Second Vatican Council and its theology of the people of God (*LG* 9–17) as well as from the conciliar statements about the relation of church and culture (*GS* 53–62). There is evidence that the essential concerns of Pope Francis are embryonically laid out already early by Pope John XXIII and then are clearly expressed in John's speech for the opening of the Council.[9] An additional impetus was the Apostolic Exhortation of Pope Paul VI, *Evangelii nuntiandi*, concerning evangelization in the world of today (1975); in it the relation of evangelization and culture is likewise thematized (*EN* 20). In the same year in which *Evangelii nuntiandi* was published, the Apostolic Exhortation *Gaudete in Domino* (Rejoice in the Lord) appeared, although it did not receive much attention from us. The topic of Pope Francis' text *Evangelii gaudium* (The Joy of the Gospel) was thereby sketched out.

Paul VI, despite all of the differences in background and personality, is for Francis the pope who is closest to him among his predecessors. His communicative dialogical style picks up many things from the encyclical *Ecclesiam suam* (1964). In his positions on social ethics, he appeals many times to Pope Paul VI's significant social encyclical *Populorum progressio* (1967) (EG 180, 219) and to his Apostolic Exhortation *Octogesima adveniens* (1971) (EG 184, 190). It was certainly deliberately intended that the beatification of Montini—Pope Paul—provided the conclusion to the new pontificate's first synod of bishops. Indeed, it was not without reason that in his homily he spoke of a courageous, humble and prophetic, far-sighted, wise, and at times lonely witness, who also served the church through his suffering.[10] Thus in the pontificate of Pope Francis, the spirit of the Second Vatican Council is coming alive again in a new and fresh way. Pope Francis is the first pope who himself did not participate in the Second Vatican Council. With his pontificate we have entered into a new phase of the postconciliar age and of conciliar reception.

Jorge Mario Bergoglio has internalized all of the diverse currents we have named. Nevertheless, he doesn't let himself be categorized into a particular school of thought. He is a man of encounter and praxis who is averse to every limited ideology. For him reality takes primacy over idea (EG 231–33). His rich knowledge of life is indebted not to theological books, but to his great pastoral experience as spiritual adviser, provincial, and bishop in the midst of the culture of Buenos Aires, which bears both a European and a specifically Argentine stamp, and in the context of its bleak slums. In addition, the world of film and classical as well as modern music and literature contributes to this knowledge. He mentions Manzoni, Dostoevsky, Hopkins, and others.[11] All of those things are sources that Pope Francis draws upon and that he has processed independently in his personal, spiritual, and pastoral experience.

The question that he faces is this: How can one cope with all of the tensions of such a multicultural world, with its contradictions, but also with its richness, and do justice to reality? Fundamental for his intellectual processing of this diverse, or as he says, polyhedral reality (*EG* 236), which cannot be reduced to a common denominator, was his engagement with Romano Guardini (1895–1968), especially during the time of his multiple-month stay in Germany in 1986. In his early work, *Der Gegensatz: Versuche einer Philosophie des lebendig Konkreten* (1925), Romano Guardini speaks of the polar tensions that mark all of life. They cannot be sublated into a speculative synthesis in Hegel's sense. The question, therefore, is, In this new pluralistic, multicultural world, how is a holistic, truly Catholic perspective possible—a perspective that is neither an ideology that co-opts everything, nor a disjointed sum of individual truths and commandments?

Whoever wants to understand the pope's answer to this question has to proceed from the fact that Jorge Bergoglio/Pope Francis is a deeply spiritual human being, to whom a particular kind of mysticism is not foreign (*EG* 82). The pope is convinced that we can understand and handle our multifaceted and conflictive reality ultimately only in light of the gospel. He knows that spiritually nothing is possible in the church and in the world without time for prayer and worship (*EG* 262). As Pope Francis says in an addendum—one that certainly derives from him—to the already prepared encyclical *Lumen fidei*, faith is a light that allows reality to be seen as what it is. Faith admittedly is "not a light that dispels all of our darkness, but rather a lamp that guides our steps in the night and that is sufficient."[12]

Only with this statement have we finally arrived at the fundamental concern of Pope Francis, which he presents in his programmatic Apostolic Exhortation *Evangelii gaudium*. In his contextual theology, he wants to shed light on the situation of the church and of Christians in the contemporary world from the perspective of the gospel. In so doing, Christian faith is not an ideology that intends to explain everything; it is not to be compared with a floodlight that illuminates the entire path of our life. Rather, it is like a lantern that shines for us on the path of life as far as we ourselves are advancing. It is a forever surprising, never exhaustible message of joy.

IV

THE GOSPEL: ORIGIN, FOUNDATION, AND SOURCE OF JOY

Pope Francis pursues matters to their root. He begins radically, that is, he begins at the root (*radix*): he begins with the gospel. Spiritual reading of sacred Scripture and reflecting upon it, which is recommended by the Second Vatican Council (*DV* 21–26), is essential for him (*EG* 174–75), as his sermons and speeches show. By *gospel* Francis does not mean a book or the four books that we call the four Gospels. For *gospel* originally does not mean a writing or a book, but a message—more precisely, the delivering of a good and liberating message, which fundamentally changes the situation, confronts the listener with a new situation, and calls him or her to a decision.

In the Old Testament, good news is the message of the imminent return of the people Israel from Babylonian captivity; in the New Testament, it is Jesus' own message of the coming of God's kingdom and the message of Jesus the Christ, of his death and his resurrection as the exalted Lord who is effectively present in the church and in the world through his Spirit; it is the message of hope for his final coming and of the dawn and gift of new life.[1] So what matters to Francis is the good news of God, which is proclaimed, believed, celebrated, and lived in a spirited way in the church. For him it is a gospel of joy in the sense of a holistic fulfillment of life that God alone, who is all in all, can give (*EG* 4–5, 265).

Already the first few sections of *Evangelii gaudium* show that the joy of the gospel is not primarily a matter of overcoming social injustice, however much this is very near and dear to Francis, as later sections make clear. The starting point lies much deeper. It concerns the lack of joy and the lack of spark, the inner emptiness and the isolation of human persons closed up in themselves and the loneliness of hearts turned in on themselves (*EG* 1–2). The image of the heart turned in on itself (*cor incurvatum*) is a well-known motif in Augustine and Luther that describes the situation of the unredeemed human being. Francis connects with this idea in his talk about self-referentiality. Ultimately, his talk about the lack of joy and energy traces back to what, from the early desert fathers up to Thomas Aquinas, is regarded as the basic sin and original temptation of human beings: the *acedia*, the indolence of the heart, the gravitational pull dragging one down, the sluggishness, the weariness in spiritual matters that leads to the unhappiness of this world (1 Cor 7:10) (*EG* 1–2, 81).[2]

This analysis of our time is not an admittedly well-intentioned, pious, yet unconvincing thought experiment. Pope Francis does not stand alone in making such an analysis. Similar analyses are found in many of the significant and authoritative thinkers of the past century. Already Søren Kierkegaard and then somewhat differently Romano Guardini have spoken of melancholy; Martin Heidegger spoke of anxiety as our basic disposition; Jean Paul Sartre, of the ennui of the contemporary human person. Friedrich Nietzsche has ironically described the "last human being," who contents himself with small, banal good fortune, for whom, however, no star shines any more. "What is love? What is creation?

What is longing? What is a star?—thus asks the last human being and blinks."[3] In a clear-sighted way, one of my predecessors in the episcopal seat of Rottenburg, Bishop Paul Wilhelm Keppler (1852–1926) emphasized with many quotations and observations the joylessness of the modern human person in the book *More Joy*, which was published in many editions and translations.[4]

Evangelii gaudium grasps the problem of the church and the contemporary world at its root. It responds to the need of our age and the crisis in the church with the gospel. The gospel is the origin, given once for all times, the enduring basis, as well as the ever-effervescent source of all Christian teaching and the discipline of morals (*DH* 1501). Only from the perspective of the gospel can faith and Christian life regain its freshness (*EG* 11). The joy of the gospel can awaken anew joy in life, in creation, in faith, and in the church. Only joy as a gift of the Holy Spirit (Rom 14:17; 15:13, among others), the joy of a "spirit-filled evangelization" (*EG* 259–61) can lead to a new awakening. Because God is the highest good, is all in all, and is gracious, joy—as the holistic fulfillment of the human person—is, according to Thomas, born of the love of God.[5]

With this approach, Francis moves in a great tradition. In the history of the church, the gospel stood in the background of many movements of renewal, beginning with the monasticism of the early church up to the reform movements of the Middle Ages. Best known is the evangelical movement of Saint Francis of Assisi and Saint Dominic. Together with his brothers, Francis simply wanted to live the gospel *sine glossa*, without addition or subtraction (cf. *EG* 271).[6] The two most significant theologians of the Middle Ages, Thomas Aquinas (1225–1274) and Bonaventure (1221–1274), emerge out of the evangelical movement of that time.

In Thomas Aquinas's *Summa theologiae* we find an article of surprising originality concerning the new law of the gospel, to which Pope Francis refers explicitly in *Evangelii gaudium* (EG 37, 43). In this article, Thomas explains that the gospel is not a written law or a code of doctrines and commandments, but rather is the inner gift of the Holy Spirit, which is given to us in faith and is active in love. Writings and regulations belong only secondarily to the gospel; they are supposed to direct us to the gift of grace or to make it effective. However, they have no independent grace-mediating significance, and that means they have no independent significance for justification.[7]

With this theology of the gospel, Thomas Aquinas and Martin Luther stand much closer to each other in this matter than it appears at first blush. For Martin Luther too, Christianity is not a religion of the book, as it was often understood in the later history of Protestantism with its appeal to "Scripture alone." The gospel is the living word of proclamation.[8] Because of mistakes on all sides and because of historical entanglements, Christianity unfortunately came to be divided over this issue in the sixteenth century.

The Council of Trent (1545–1563), which engaged in debate with the teaching of the Reformers, was not blind to evangelical concerns (understood in the original sense of that word). Already in its first dogmatic decree, the Council declared that it wanted to preserve and to reestablish the purity of the gospel. And by that it meant the gospel as it is preached, believed, and lived in the church, as the living source of every truth of salvation and moral doctrine.[9] On this basis, Trent introduced a renewal of the church and, in one of its first reform decrees, it identified preaching as the primary task of the bishop.[10] Saint Charles Borromeo, who is regarded as a model post-Tridentine reform bishop, became for Angelo Roncalli, the later John XXIII, the role model in this matter, even for his idea of a council.[11]

At the Second Vatican Council, the book of the Gospels was solemnly enthroned before the Council fathers at every session so that the gospel should have pride of place. The Council has then once again moved the proclaimed and lived word of God into the center of the church's life (*DV* 7, 21–26; *LG* 23–25). In *Evangelii nuntiandi*, Paul VI described evangelization as the essential mission of the church, indeed as its deepest identity (*EN* 14), and he spoke of the necessity of the church's own self-evangelization (*EN* 15). John Paul II, in numerous addresses and, in summary fashion, in his encyclical about mission, *Redemptoris missio* (1990), unfolded the program of a new evangelization. Benedict XVI took up this concern in his Apostolic Letter *Porta fidei* (2011) and with the bishops' synod of 2012. The fruit of the synod was adopted in many places in the Apostolic Exhortation *Evangelii gaudium* (*EG* 1, 14–15, 262–83). Thus evangelization became *the* pastoral program of the church, also and especially under Pope Francis.[12]

Pope Francis stands in a tradition that reaches back to the very beginnings, but he stands especially in the tradition of his immediate predecessors. At the same time, he stands in the center of our time. For in the aporias of the present, modernity threatens to peter out in the West in postmodernity, while fatal economic consequences for millions of people work themselves out in the southern sphere of our globe. In this situation many are searching for an alternative, and they find it increasingly in evangelical movements. Observers in the Catholic Church of the twenty-first century have also detected this evangelical trend.[13]

Pope Francis has understood this heartbeat of the contemporary church. He does not represent a liberal position, but rather a radical one—understood in the original sense of the word—that is, a position that goes back to the root (*radix*). This return to the origin, however, is no retreat into yesterday or the day before yesterday; rather, it is power for a bold emergence into tomorrow. With his gospel program, he seizes upon the original message of the church as well as the fundamental need of the present, and he launches a fundamental renewal. In this way, he does not fit either into a traditionalist or a progressive scheme. By building a bridge to the origin, he is a bridge builder into the future.

The gospel is a good but also a challenging message. It is a call to conversion and a new orientation. In the process, it necessarily arouses resistance. So too the pope's talk of the gospel has made many uneasy. Pope Francis talks a lot about the gospel, but noticeably little about the church's doctrine. Therefore many a person asks how he relates to the doctrine of the church. Does he even intend to bring the gospel and doctrine into opposition, as liberal theology has done?[14]

Naturally, Pope Francis does not intend to adopt this liberal understanding. On the contrary, as the Council of Trent already stated, the gospel is the source from which doctrines originate.[15] For Francis that is not only a historical statement. From this historical observation, rather, it follows that one has to interpret doctrine in the light of the gospel. Pope Francis draws this conclusion. He recollects anew the teaching of the Second Vatican Council concerning the hierarchy of truths. It requires that the church's many and diverse truths be interpreted from their christological foundation and from their christological center (*UR* 11; *EG* 36).[16]

This teaching is not new. Already Thomas Aquinas had made clear that the faith is not an extraneous aggregate of all sorts of truths, but rather that every statement is a member of an articulated whole (*articulus fidei*).[17] He knew that the basic articles of faith imply the entirety of the gospel.[18] The First Vatican Council thus demanded that the faith be understood from the inner connection of the mysteries of faith and with a view to the final goal of human beings (*DH* 3016). There is a hierarchy not only of truths, but also of virtues.[19] Catholic moral teaching is not a catalog of sins and mistakes. All virtues are at the service of the response of love (*EG* 39). Jesus himself summarizes the law and the prophets in the chief commandment of love of God and love of neighbor (Matt 22:34–40; cf. 5:43; Rom 13:8–10; Gal 5:14).

Pope Francis describes as the "basic core the beauty of the saving love of God made manifest in Jesus Christ, who died and rose from the dead" (EG 36). He draws practical conclusions for preaching from this insight. He says that in preaching one may not reduce doctrine to its secondary aspects, but rather must understand it in context, from the center of the message of Jesus Christ (EG 34–39; 246). Only if one sees the truths of faith in their inner connection can one make them shine anew in their original beauty and in their complete attractiveness. Only in this way can the fragrance of the gospel be disseminated anew (EG 34, 39).

This kerygmatic program approximates Luther's tenet, "what promotes Christ,"[20] but is still very different from it, because for the Council and for Pope Francis, it is not a question of an *exclusive* principle with which one can exclude so-called secondary and unwieldy truths or can write them off as less binding. For Pope Francis it has to do with an *inclusive* hermeneutical principle and, in the process, it has to do above all with the pastoral concern of preaching, with whose assistance he wants to understand and let shine anew the full and complete gospel in its inner beauty (EG 237).[21]

Pope Francis does not want to revolutionize faith and morals; he wants to interpret faith and morals from the perspective of the gospel. Corresponding to the proclamation character of the gospel, he does that, not in an abstract, didactic manner of speech, but rather in a simple, but not simplistic, communicative and dialogical manner of speech that speaks to people. In the process, he surrenders nothing of doctrine. Rather, in this way he can show that the faith is an ever-fresh and refreshing wellspring (EG 11) and is a truth that never goes out of fashion (EG 265). His motive is to convince the faithful of the beauty of faith and encourage them to living joyfully the life of faith.

V

MERCY—THE KEY WORD
OF HIS PONTIFICATE

For Pope Francis, the message of mercy stands in the center of the gospel. Already as bishop, his episcopal coat of arms proclaimed the motto *Miserando et eligendo* (by gazing upon me with the eyes of his mercy, he has chosen me), following Bede the Venerable (seventh–eighth century). The topic of mercy has now become the key word of his pontificate, a topic that, from the very first day, he addresses over and over again in countless speeches. He says repeatedly that God's mercy is infinite; God will never tire of being merciful toward everyone if only we do not tire of asking for his mercy. God forsakes no person and lets none fall (*EG* 3). A little mercy among human beings can change the world.[1] With this theme he has touched the hearts of countless people inside as well as outside of the church. For who among us would not rely on a merciful God and on merciful fellow human beings?

Mercy is a central biblical theme.[2] Already in the Old Testament God is not only the God who punishes and avenges. In the revelation to Moses we hear, "YHWH is a merciful and gracious God" (Exod 34:6). The prophets and the Psalms repeat this statement time and again: "The Lord is merciful and gracious, slow to anger and abounding in steadfast love" (Pss 103:8; 111:4). Downright dramatically, the prophet Hosea expresses the sovereignty of God in his mercy, who forgives the people and grants them a new beginning despite their infidelity: "My compassion grows warm and tender…for I am God and no mortal" (Hos 11:8–9).

The mercy of God is altogether pivotal in Jesus' message. Let us think only of the parable of the prodigal son, which we should better describe as the parable of the merciful father (Luke 15:11–32), or of the parable of the good Samaritan (Luke 10:25–37), or of the statement in the Letter to the Ephesians: "God, who is rich in mercy" (Eph 2:4). In addition, let us think of the Beatitudes of the Sermon on the Mount: "Blessed are the merciful" (Matt 5:7), or the statement "For I desire steadfast love [mercy] and not sacrifice" (Hos 6:6; Matt 9:13; 12:7), or Jesus' speech about the last judgment, according to which only the works of mercy count (Matt 25:31–45).

It is all the more surprising that Scholastic theology has neglected this topic and turned it into a mere subordinate theme of justice. Scholastic theology thereby has gotten tangled up in great difficulties. For when one makes justice the higher criterion, the question arises how a just God, who must punish evil and reward good, can be merciful and grant pardon. Isn't that unfair to those who have striven in an upright manner to live a good life?

Drawing upon Anselm of Canterbury, Thomas Aquinas was smart enough to see that God is not bound to our rules of justice. God is sovereign; he is just in relation to himself, who is love (1 John 4:8, 16). Because God is love and therein is faithful to himself, he is also merciful. Mercy is the aspect of God's essence that is turned outward.[3] It is the fidelity of God to himself and the expression of his absolute sovereignty in love.[4]

One could also say that as God's fidelity to himself, mercy is simultaneously God's fidelity to his covenant and is his steadfast forbearance with human beings. In his mercy, God leaves no one in the lurch. Divine mercy gives everyone a new chance and grants everyone a new beginning, if he or she is eager for conversion and asks for it. Mercy is God's own justice, which does not condemn the sinner who wants to be converted, but rather makes him or her just. Let it, however, be understood: mercy justifies the sinner, not the sin. The commandment of mercy also wants the church not to make life difficult for the faithful and to make religion a form of servitude. Mercy wills—so says Thomas Aquinas, citing Augustine—that we be free of oppressive burdens (*EG* 43).[5] It is the basis for the joy that the gospel bestows (*EG* 2–8).

With this message, Pope Francis stands in the tradition of many great saints (such as Catherine of Siena, Thérèse de Lisieux, and others). Already for John XXIII, mercy was the most beautiful of all the divine attributes.[6] In his famous speech at the opening of the Second Vatican Council on October 11, 1962, he warned that the church today must no longer make use of the weapons of severity, but must rather apply the medicine of mercy. In this way, John XXIII already set the basic tone for the conciliar and post-conciliar time and its new pastoral orientation.

In light of his experience of the horrors of the Second World War, the Shoah, the Nazi era, and the communist era in Poland, Pope John Paul II came to realize the message of mercy. Thus he devoted his second encyclical *Dives in misericordia* (1980) to this topic. Later he took up the suggestions of Sister Faustina Kowalska and made the Sunday after Easter Mercy Sunday. In the Jubilee Year 2000, he programmatically canonized Sister Faustina as the first saint in the new millennium.[7] Benedict XVI carried this theme forward and deepened it theologically in his first encyclical *Deus caritas est* (2005).

Pope Francis again connects originality with continuity and continuity with originality when it is a question of concrete pastoral application. He said it quite directly to the Argentine youth on July 25, 2013 in Rio de Janeiro:

> Look, read the beatitudes, which will do you good. If you then want to know what you concretely must do, read Matthew chapter 25. That is the model according to which we are judged. With these two things you have an action plan: the beatitudes and Matthew 25. You don't need to read anything else. I ask you to do this from the bottom of my heart.

Despite this unambiguous grounding in Scripture and tradition, many a person finds the pope's talk of mercy suspect. They confuse mercy with superficial laissez-faire pseudomercy and, when they hear of mercy, they perceive the danger that what is being spoken of thereby is a weaker, pastoral permissiveness and a Christianity-lite, a way of being Christian at a reduced cost.[8] So they see in mercy a kind of "fabric softener" that undermines the dogmas and commandments and abrogates the central and fundamental meaning of truth.

That is an accusation that the Pharisees made against Jesus. Jesus' mercy so enraged them that they decided to kill him (Matt 12:1–8, 9–14). Moreover, that is a gross misunderstanding of the deep biblical sense of mercy. For mercy is itself a fundamental truth of revelation and a demanding and challenging commandment of Jesus. It stands in an inner connection with all of the other truths of revelation and commandments. Rightly understood, how is it, therefore, supposed to put into question the truth and the commandments? It also does not abolish justice, but rather surpasses it. It is the higher righteousness, without which no one can enter the kingdom of heaven (Matt 5:20). To pit mercy against the truth or against the commandments and to bring them into opposition to each other is, therefore, theologically nonsensical. In contrast, it is right to understand mercy, which is the fundamental attribute of God and the greatest of all the virtues (EG 37), in the sense of the hierarchy of truths as the hermeneutical principle, not to replace or to undermine doctrine and the commandments, but rather to understand and to actualize them in the right way, according to the gospel.

One can also characterize this highlighting of mercy—as a foundational hermeneutical principle—as a paradigm shift: from a deductive method to a method in the sense of see-judge-act, which begins inductively at first and, only in a second step, introduces theological criteria. Such a paradigm shift can elicit irritations and misunderstandings like the ones just mentioned, as if what had been previously said was no longer valid. However, rightly understood, the paradigm shift does not change the previously valid content of what has been taught, but certainly changes the perspective and the horizon in which it is seen and understood. Already Pope Paul VI referred to the new perspective when, in his speech during the last session of the Second Vatican Council on December 7, 1965, he described the example of the good Samaritan as the Council's model of spirituality. With this parable Jesus intends to give an answer to the question, Who is my neighbor? His answer is not deductive, but rather inductive in that it proceeds from the concrete human situation. Your neighbor is the one whom you encounter who, in a concrete situation, is in need of your help and your mercy, to whom you must bend low and bind his or her wounds. The neighbor is for you the exposition of the concrete will of God (Luke 10:25–37).

The challenge of this new paradigm stretches wide and goes deep. For if mercy is the most fundamental of all divine attributes, then through it the most fundamental of all theological questions—the question of God—is posed anew. We cannot pursue it here in this context.[9] Here we are concerned with the concrete conclusions at which Pope Francis arrives. When Jesus says, "Be merciful, just as your Father is merciful" (Luke 6:36), then that has far-reaching consequences for the shaping of Christian life through corporal and spiritual works of mercy.[10] Talk of God's mercy is, therefore, no pretty yet harmless cliché. It does not gently rock us in a deceptive tranquility and security; it causes us to get moving. It wants us to open our hands and, above all, open our hearts. For *misericordia* means having a heart for the poor, the poor in the widest and most comprehensive sense. In the final two chapters, we will return explicitly to its consequences for Christian ethics, especially for social ethics.

But first, it is a question of the ramifications of talk about mercy for the understanding and praxis of the church. For if we are supposed to be merciful as our Father in heaven is merciful, then that is valid not only for the individual believer, but also for the church. The church is and is supposed to be the sacrament— that is, the sign and instrument—of God's mercy. To this topic we must now turn.

VI

PEOPLE-OF-GOD ECCLESIOLOGY UNDERSTOOD CONCRETELY

The Bible and the tradition know various images for describing the essence of the church.[1] In the center of Pope Francis' understanding of the church, corresponding to the approach of the Argentine theology of the people, stands the image of the church as the people of God (*EG* 111–34). It is firmly anchored in the biblical, patristic, and liturgical tradition.[2] The Second Vatican Council has again renewed this understanding and has presented the church as the messianic people of God (*LG* 9–12).[3] However, before long reservations grew loud in European theology. One suspected a one-sided sociological, political, grassroots ecclesiology.[4] It was different in Argentina. There the impulse of the Council was eagerly seized upon and further developed into the Argentine form of liberation theology, into the theology of the people. Pope Francis imbues this ecclesiology of the people of God with concrete life.[5]

That is not a new, but is certainly a renewed view of the church, which should lead to a new style of ecclesial life. Pope Francis speaks in *Evangelii gaudium* of "pastoral care in conversion," that is, *Bekehrung* (Spanish *conversión*; Italian *conversione*), which only the German translation, in distinction from all other translations that I can understand, communicates quite blandly as "reorientation" (*EG* 25). We should not water down the strong words of the pope; rather, we should let them stand as they are and take them seriously. In his speech to the bishops of Brazil in Rio de Janeiro, he said very clearly what is meant by this pastoral conversion:

> In reference to the conversion in pastoral care, I would like to remind you that "pastoral care" is nothing other than the exercise of the church's motherhood. She gives birth, breastfeeds, lets grow, corrects, nourishes, leads by the hand....There is need therefore for a church that is capable of rediscovering the womb of mercy. Without mercy it is scarcely possible today to penetrate into a world of the "injured," who need understanding, forgiveness, and love.

One can correctly understand Pope Francis' style against the background of the theology of the people. This style is not good-natured folksiness or even cheap populism. Behind the pope's pastoral style, which is close to the people, stands an entire theology, indeed his mysticism of the people. For him the church is far more than an organic and hierarchical institution. It is above all the people of God on their way to God, a pilgrim and evangelizing people that transcends every—even if necessary—institutional expression.

Ultimately, the church is rooted in the secret of the most holy Trinity. Salvation is a work of God's mercy. Out of sheer grace God draws us to himself through his Spirit and brings us together as his people. Thus, the church stands under the primacy of grace; the Lord always precedes us with his love and his initiative (*EG* 24). Through his Spirit he draws us to himself, not as isolated individuals, but as his people. So the church must be the place of renegotiated mercy, where all can feel themselves welcomed and loved, where they experience pardon and can feel encouraged to live according to the good life of the gospel (*EG* 111–14).

On the basis of his theology of the people of God, Pope Francis is averse to every form of clericalism. "Lay people are, put simply, the vast majority of the people of God. The minority— ordained ministers—are at their service" (*EG* 102). The shepherds should not feel that they are fine, genteel lords, but rather should take on the smell of the sheep (*EG* 24). Francis wants the participation of the entire people of God in the life of the church—women as well as men, lay people as well as clerics, young and old. On the basis of baptism and confirmation, all are missionary disciples; they should be included in decisions. Lay ministries certainly ought not be restricted to intraecclesial tasks; they are supposed to have an impact on advancing Christian values in the social, political, and economic world and should be engaged in applying the gospel to the transformation of society. The education of the laity and the evangelization of the professional and intellectual life pose, therefore, a significant pastoral challenge (*EG* 102, 119–34).

The topic of women is especially important to the pope; he devotes two sections to them in *Evangelii gaudium* (*EG* 103–4). Already John XXIII counted the participation of women in public life and consciousness raising concerning their human dignity among the signs of the times.[6] Pope Francis recognizes that women make an indispensable contribution in society and he joyfully notes how many women exercise pastoral responsibility in the church, together with priests. "But we need to create still broader opportunities for a more incisive female presence in the Church. Because 'the feminine genius is indispensable in all forms of expressions of the life of society'" (*EG* 103).[7] All the same, the reservation of the priesthood to men, as a sign of Christ, the bridegroom who offers himself in the Eucharist, is not open to discussion. However, in the case of sacramental power, we are moving on the plane of function and not of dignity or superiority.[8] "Indeed, a woman, Mary, is more important than the bishops."

For Pope Francis that is not a defensive argument. Rather, he sees in it "a great challenge for pastors and theologians"; it is a matter of recognizing more fully "what this entails with regard to the possible role of women in decision-making in different areas of the Church's life" (EG 104). There are, in fact, many influential positions in the church, including the Roman Curia, which do not require ordination and are open to women, where women could introduce their specific talents for the well-being of the church and could break up an all too one-sided clerical atmosphere simply through their presence and their collaboration.

Young people are important to the pope—one might almost say, as a matter of course. In his welcoming address at World Youth Day in Rio de Janeiro on July 25, 2013, he said,

> I have come as well to be confirmed by the enthusiasm of your faith. You know that in the life of a Bishop there are many problems that need to be resolved. And with these problems and difficulties, a Bishop's faith can grow sad. How horrible is a sad Bishop! How bad is that! So that my faith might not be sad, I came here to be filled with your contagious enthusiasm!

Pope Francis knows—again one might say, as a matter of course—about the difficulties of young people today and the difficulties of youth ministry (EG 105–6). But he also knows that "young people call us to renewed and expansive hope, for they represent new directions for humanity and open us up to the future, lest we cling to a nostalgia for structures and customs which are no longer life-giving in today's world" (EG 108).

The pope names the theological foundation of the significance of the laity's witness in the church. He refers to the teaching of the *sensus fidei*, the spiritual sense for what is a matter of faith and living the life of faith. The doctrine of *sensus fidei*, which is imparted to every Christian through the Holy Spirit in baptism, is very well established in the biblical and theological tradition, but has often been neglected. John Henry Newman showcased it in a renewed way in his famous essay, "On Consulting the Faithful in Matters of Doctrine,"[9] and the last Council has renewed it again. It states that the people of God as a whole cannot err in matters of belief (*LG* 12; *EG* 119, 139, 198).[10]

Unfortunately, this teaching has again been neglected after the Council. There was a fear that it would be misused by dissent groups inside the church. Pope Francis doesn't share these fears. He brings the doctrine of the *sensus fidei* out again and also draws from it the necessary conclusion by saying that the church must keep its ear to the people (*EG* 154). He speaks of the laity's instinct for finding new ways of evangelization and he argues, therefore, in favor of making provisions for their voice and for pastoral dialogue (*EG* 31).

Pope Francis wants a magisterium that listens. He shows how serious he is in *Evangelii gaudium*. In this Apostolic Exhortation, he cites not only statements from the Roman magisterium, but very often he also cites documents from episcopal conferences from around the world. Popular piety is especially important to him. It is a fruit of the Holy Spirit, a theological source (*locus theologicus*) and is, so to speak, the mother tongue of the faith (*EG* 69–70, 90, 122–26). The *Aparecida Document* speaks of the "people's mysticism" (cited in *EG* 124, 237).

All of that does not mean that the church creates out of itself the truth and its vital power. On the contrary, as the itinerant people of God, the church does not live out of its own resources, but rather from listening to the word of God and from the sacraments, especially the Eucharist. The pope devotes the entire, lengthy third chapter of *Evangelii gaudium* to living on the basis of the proclaimed word of God.

> All evangelization is based on that word, listened to, meditated upon, lived, celebrated and witnessed to…. The Church does not evangelize unless she constantly lets herself be evangelized. It is indispensable that the word of God be ever more fully at the heart of every ecclesial activity. God's word, listened to and celebrated, above all in the Eucharist, nourishes and inwardly strengthens Christians, enabling them to offer an authentic witness to the Gospel in daily life….The preaching of the word, living and effective, prepares for the reception of the sacrament, and in the sacrament that word attains its maximum efficacy. (*EG* 174)

Also in reference to the sacraments, the church is a merciful mother with an open heart for all. The sacraments are medicine and nourishment for the weak; they are not only for the perfect (*EG* 47). The church should be an open house with open doors (*EG* 46–49). It seems that Francis prefers the image of the church as a merciful mother, which was dear to the martyr-bishop Cyprian in his dispute with Novatian, to Novatian's image of the church as a pure and holy virgin. Against the rigorism of Novatian, Cyprian supported the cause of clemency and mercy for those Christians who had become weak during persecution (*lapsi*). Today Pope Francis says that he prefers a church that is bruised, hurting, and dirty because it has been out on the streets, rather than a church remaining shut up within its structures, while outside a starving multitude is waiting (*EG* 49).[11]

With these and many other statements in the pope's daily homilies in St. Martha, it appears to many that the pope has laid the groundwork for allowing Christians in irregular situations, such as divorced and remarried individuals, after examination of their respective situation, to the sacraments of reconciliation and Eucharist. The pope has responded that he was not thinking of such concrete situations when he made his general statement in *Evangelii gaudium*. Until there is a decision about the pastorally pressing, yet still contentiously discussed question, he wants, in the exercise of his office of unity, first to hear what the Spirit is saying to the churches (Rev 2:7, 11, 17, 29, etc.) and then decide.

In my talk before the consistory, contrary to many misrepresentations, I touched upon the question just mentioned, but intentionally left it open and expressly referred to the decision of the synod in communion with the pope.[12] "Remaining in the truth" is for me, as for all of the theologians who took part in the discussion, a matter of course. The question that awaits a decision, however, is what does truth mean in the sense of the biblical truth of divine faithfulness (*emet*) in a concrete situation.[13] This question, as many recent exegetical investigations show, cannot be decided merely by quoting the words of Jesus (Mark 10:2–12 and parallels), which were transmitted differently already in the New Testament.[14] Even if the question under consideration is not the only, nor even the central question of the family in the present context, it has nonetheless become for many Christians the test of the viability of the new pastoral style. Therefore, it is to be hoped that in keeping with the old conciliar tradition, after all have been heard, a great consensus about it can be achieved so that, unified, we can turn all the more to the fundamental questions in the present crisis of the family (*EG* 66–67).

For this reason it would be wrong to stay fixated on internal ecclesial problems and on what is often characterized as "hot potatoes." Pope Francis is thinking beyond the church's inner space. Already in the preconclave period, the then Cardinal Bergoglio pointed out that the church ought not to be focused on itself; it ought not be a church that is narcissistically in love with itself and revolving around itself. A self-involved human being is a sick human being, a self-involved church is a sick church (*EG* 43).[15] Francis wants out of the stale air of a church that is self-involved—suffering from its own condition, bemoaning or celebrating itself. For him the church is an open house and a church with open doors, a father's house, in which there is a place for everyone with their difficulties (*EG* 46–49). Therefore, he warns about a fundamentalism as well as about a one-sided sacramentalization of ecclesial life (*EG* 63).

Pope Francis' paradigm for the church is mission, a pastoral ministry that is not only preservative, but rather decidedly missionary (*EG* 15), a church that is permanently in a state of mission (*EG* 25). That does not mean proselytism. The church grows not by proselytizing, but by attracting (*EG* 14). As the pope repeatedly says, concretely it is a matter of being a church that goes to the peripheries (*EG* 17, 20, 24, 30, 46). What is meant by this are not only the bleak peripheries of megalopolises, but likewise the peripheries of human existence (*EG* 20–23, 27–31, 78–86, among others).

God is a God of the journey, who has patiently traveled a long path with us in the history of salvation. The church fathers spoke of God's patience and forbearance, of his pedagogy and economy.[16] As we have already seen, the motif of a journey or path is important for Francis (*EG* 23–24). For him faith is not a fixed standpoint, but rather a path on which every individual, as well as the church as a whole, is on the way. The church's task is step by step to accompany people wisely, patiently, and mercifully on this path and this process of growth. Francis quotes Blessed Peter Faber, for whom he has special esteem: "Time is God's messenger"

(*EG* 169–73). The extraordinary synod of 2014, in its concluding document, adopted this understanding of a pastoral ministry that meets people where they are and accompanies them.

With that said, we touch upon the deepest—I would like to say the mystical—dimension of Pope Francis' ecclesiology. He wants to encounter Christ—indeed, to touch Christ—in the poor (*EG* 270). The church is the body of Christ; therefore, we touch the wounds of Christ in the wounds of the others. "Truly I tell you, just as you did it to one of the least of these who are members of my family, you did it to me" (Matt 25:40). That is a mystical point of view (*EG* 87, 92). It calls to mind Francis of Assisi who, at the beginning of his spiritual journey, embraced a leper; and it recalls Mother Teresa's experience of her calling, when she carried a dying person into her cloister and, in the process, had the experience of carrying Christ in her arms, as it were, like a monstrance. In Albania, the land of Mother Teresa's origin, on September 21, 2014 Francis—after meeting with martyrs who had suffered horrible things under the communist terror—spoke in a very moving way of a church that can administer solace because it too has experienced solace (cf. 2 Cor 1:3–5).

At this point the already mentioned paradigm shift in method, corresponding to the model of the Good Samaritan, becomes concrete.[17] The Samaritan descends into the dust and dirt of the street, touches and binds up the wounds of the one fallen among robbers, and also pays for his care. Francis speaks of a mysticism of coexistence and encounter, of embracing and supporting one another, of participating in a caravan of solidarity, in a sacred pilgrimage (*EG* 87); he speaks of a mystical and contemplative fraternity, which "knows how to see the sacred grandeur of our neighbor, of finding God in every human being" (*EG* 92). Or—to say it in the words of Johann Baptist Metz—it is not a mysticism of closed eyes, but rather a mysticism of open eyes,[18] which becomes a mysticism of hands-on, helping hands.

For Pope Francis, the guiding star of evangelization and of this kind of pastoral care, which accompanies and cares for others, is Mary, the mother of Jesus and our mother (*EG* 284–88). Having such a closing chapter devoted to Mary has become a tradition in the encyclicals of the last few popes. For a pope who comes from Latin America and is devoted to popular piety, such a chapter is completely natural. Especially Guadeloupe in Mexico, then Aparecida in Brazil, and Luchan in Argentina are Marian pilgrimage sites of national and continental significance.

We should not arrogantly dismiss their mention as a tribute to the ancestry and culture of the pope, but rather acknowledge the religious power—including the power of the new evangelization—that emanated and still emanates today from these centers in the history of the Latin American continent. We should take seriously that without Mary we can never entirely understand the spirit of the new evangelization and can never entirely understand the church as well.[19] Without Mary the church would lack a feminine image. Mary accompanies God's people on the path of evangelization, even in periods of dryness and darkness, which include many a tribulation. She is the model and advocate of evangelization. Thus, there is a Marian style in the missionary activity of the church; it is a revolution of tenderness and love (*EG* 88, 288).[20]

VII

PERSPECTIVES OF
ECCLESIAL RENEWAL

F rancis was elected pope in order to lead the church out of the
crisis that came to light in the *Vatileaks* and other scandals. A
missionary church, as Francis understands it, must be a church
that takes the path of renewal (*LG* 8; *EG* 26–27, 43, among others). Francis has resolutely seized upon this task. In this context,
what interests us are not the individual measures, such as the
reform of the Curia, which is only in the beginning phase and is
a long way from being concluded. The following has to do not
with institutional questions of curial reform, but rather with the
foundational perspectives of church reform, which is not possible
without a fundamental change in mentality. The pope does not
even shy away from speaking of a conversion of the papacy, which
the German translation unfortunately communicated very blandly
as a "new orientation" (*EG* 32).

Already on the first evening, when he appeared on the bal-
cony of St. Peter's Basilica, the new pope presented himself as
Bishop of Rome. That is one of the oldest papal titles.[1] With this
self-description, he has adopted the statement of the martyr-bishop
Ignatius of Antioch (approximately around the middle of the second century), who described the church of Rome as presiding in

love.[2] In the background stands the recollection of the ancient ecclesiology, according to which pastoral responsibility for the universal church is assigned to the bishop of Rome. To be bishop of Rome is here no appendix to the Petrine office, but rather its basis.

Behind this understanding stands the ancient church's idea of the church as *communio*, an idea that was renewed by the Second Vatican Council. Pope Francis appears to have been familiar with it primarily through Henri de Lubac's *Méditations sur l'Église*.[3] As *communio*, the church has its own constitutional structure. It is neither a federal system, in which the individual local churches affiliate themselves with the universal church, nor a centralized system, in which the local churches are provinces of the world church, dependent upon the central office. The one church is present in the local churches; in them the one church assumes a concrete form and a concrete face in that place. The one universal church exists in and from the local churches (*LG* 23); conversely, the local churches live in, with, and from the one universal church. Thus, between the world church and the local church there exists a mutual interpenetration (perichoresis).[4]

The relation of the universal and the local church was a hotly debated topic in the last few decades. Even Cardinal Bergoglio as archbishop of Buenos Aires occasionally ran into conflict about this with offices in the Roman Curia. He is now taking up the topic within the parameters of *communio* ecclesiology; he speaks of the decentralization of the church and of strengthening episcopal conferences (*EG* 16, 32). Of course, he is not calling into question the Petrine office as the visible center of the church's unity. Especially in a globalized world and considered ecumenically, the Petrine office is a gift of the Lord for his church. To feel blessed to have such a center is, however, something other than the endorsement of a one-sided Roman centralization, which, in a world of diverse cultures with legitimate autonomy (*EG* 115), cannot do justice to the legitimate, relative autonomy of local churches. "Excessive centralization, rather than proving helpful, complicates the Church's life and her missionary outreach" (*EG* 32).

So Pope Francis seizes an impulse from John Paul II's ecumenical encyclical *Ut unum sint*. Even Pope Benedict XVI had adopted this recommendation. Like both of his predecessors, Pope Francis now declares himself ready to engage in ecumenical dialogue about how the Petrine office, without surrendering its substance, should be exercised today in a way that can be generally accepted.[5] Francis notes that we have made little progress in this regard. In the original Spanish text, he calls for a conversion (*conversión*) of the papacy (*EG* 32). At the same time, he recalls the statements of the Second Vatican Council about the significance of the patriarchal churches (*LG* 23). In this sense, he has repeated the offer of dialogue during an ecumenical service of remembrance in the Church of the Holy Sepulchre in Jerusalem on May 25, 2014, a service that he celebrated together with the Ecumenical Patriarch Bartholomew and other church leaders in memory of the historic meeting of Pope Paul VI with Ecumenical Patriarch Athenagoras fifty years ago.

The decisive point is binding together collegiality—synodality—and primacy. Neither is opposed to the other, but they are supposed to complement each other. The Second Vatican Council discussed this matter at length (*LG* 22).[6] At the present moment, the renewal of the synodal principle stands above all in the foreground. The word *synod* is the combination of the two Greek words *syn* (with one another, together) and *hodòs* (way). Synodality, in a general sense, means being together on the path of the entire people of God in communion with the apostolic office.

In this sense, already the so-called Jerusalem council of the apostles sketched out the later tradition (Acts 15). Then it was a question of the transition from the original Jewish-Christian church to the world church of Jews and Gentiles—therefore, it was a question of fundamental significance for the entire further development. Initially, there were arguments. From the very beginning, controversial discussions are a part of the church just as much as is the path of finding consensus through synods. At that time, the question was unanimously decided in the Holy Spirit, under the presidency of the apostle Peter in a gathering of apostles and elders, together with the entire community.

Later, the church continued to proceed in this way to handle difficult questions that were essential for faith, either in councils or synods. In these controversies a common answer was sought and was found. That happened on the level of the universal church as well as on the local church plane. Basically, the synodal principle sank into obscurity only in the nineteenth and twentieth century because of a one-sided emphasis upon Roman primacy. With its doctrine of the collegiality of the episcopal office, the emphasis upon episcopal conferences, and the establishment of pastoral councils, the Second Vatican Council has made a new beginning, which it is necessary to develop further. The synodal principle always remained alive in the churches of the East. The *Ravenna Document* (2007) has attempted a first step toward an agreement, which was expressly welcomed by Pope Francis.[7] Unfortunately, this text has been rejected by the Moscow patriarchate. Nonetheless, the Catholic-Orthodox Commission continues to work undeterred on this topic.

Pope Francis now wants to strengthen the synodal elements in the Catholic Church itself. That is supposed to happen on all levels of the local churches as well as on the level of the universal church. At the universal level, it is, above all, a matter of strengthening the synod of bishops. At the suggestion of the Second Vatican Council (CD 5), the synod of bishops was established by Pope

Paul VI with his Motu proprio *Apostolica sollicitudo* (1965) as a representation of the entire episcopate and as an expression of its universal responsibility with and under the Petrine office. However, with all of the progress achieved in the meantime, the church up to now has still remained in its first tentative steps with regard to the synod of bishops. Most recently, a certain dissatisfaction has been registered with the process, which heretofore had become somewhat sterile. That shows that we must go beyond what has already been achieved.

Pope Francis has taken a first step with the convocation of the synod on "Pastoral Challenges for the Family in the Context of Evangelization." More appropriately, one should speak of a *synodal process* rather than of a synod. It began with a questionnaire; it should be accompanied by prayer at family pilgrimage sites and later by a congress on the family. The extraordinary synod of bishops in fall 2014 was only supposed to clarify the state of the question—that is, gather the questions. Afterward, there is supposed to be an entire year for deliberations about the questions in local churches and in episcopal conferences. Only after that is the ordinary synod in fall 2015 supposed to summarize the consultations and, together with the pope, make decisions.

That is a process-oriented, dialogical style, in which the entire people of God should be involved. It has nothing to do with a democratic constitution or even with a plebiscite. It is not a matter of decisions being made by the majority, but rather a matter of communal listening to what the Spirit is saying to the communities (Rev 2:7, 11, 17, 29, among others). In listening to the multifarious voices in the church and in the exchange of everyone's testimonies to faith, in the Holy Spirit the one voice of the gospel should get a chance to speak. The decisive word in the discernment of spirits remains with the bishops and with the special charism of truth that is conferred upon them through consecration.[8] What's more, a magisterium that listens remains a magisterium that is competent to make decisions. As Pope Francis has made clear at the end of the extraordinary synod with words from the First and Second Vatican Councils, in the end the synod of bishops and, in particular, the pope will decide.

The synodal process gives expression to the idea that the church is a unity in the multiplicity of local churches, of communities in the church, and of charisms. In his sermon in the Cathedral of the Holy Spirit in Istanbul on November 29, 2014, the pope very powerfully handled the topic of the church's unity in a multiplicity of charisms that is effected by the one Spirit of God. Unity in diversity makes clear that the church is not a closed system that can be led by one single immanent point in the system or by one single authority. In the church there is an interplay of different charisms, ministries, and offices, which is beyond human control but is led by the Spirit of God. These different charisms, ministries, and offices have their own respective function. Neither can the synod replace or overrule papal primacy nor can papal primacy exclude the collegiality and synodality of the church. All depend upon working together with each other.[9] That is—according to Johann Adam Möhler—the idea of the Catholic Church.[10]

VIII

ECUMENICAL VISION

U nity and diversity: with this tensive unity, the ecumenical problem and the ecumenical vision of Pope Francis is also broached. With his election as pope, some may have thought that, being a bishop from Latin America, which is commonly regarded as a Catholic continent, little indeed was to be expected with regard to ecumenism. However, whoever was familiar with Cardinal Bergoglio knew that ecumenical concerns were close to his heart already as archbishop of Buenos Aires. Proof of that is evident in his friendly closeness with the Orthodox metropolitanate and with the Lutheran community in Buenos Aires, and especially, his familiarity, which has grown over the years, with Pentecostal churches, which are not only booming in Latin America.

Already at his first meeting with representatives of the churches and ecclesial communities immediately following his solemn installation, the new pope confirmed his intention to champion, following the line of his predecessors, but with "still greater emphasis the full realization of God's plan and to advance ecumenical dialogue."[1] In *Evangelii gaudium* three sections are devoted to ecumenism (244–46; cf. 99–101, 131). At first glance they contain what is already well-known and little that is new. But they are nevertheless important simply because they dispel all ecumenical doubt and are a clear acknowledgment of the fundamental ecumenical concern of the Second Vatican Council and its Decree on Ecumenism, *Unitatis redintegratio*, whose fiftieth anniversary we celebrated in 2014.

Ecumenism had made much progress since the Second Vatican Council. On the personal level and in collaboration, many things had evolved on all levels. The documents of theological dialogue showed significant convergence concerning many questions, albeit not full unity. In the most recent years, however, stagnation and weariness were to be seen on all sides, as well as deficient reception of the results that had been achieved. And heretofore unknown new difficulties, especially in ethical questions with our Protestant partners, who were disturbed for a long time by the unnecessarily harsh formulations in the Congregation for the Doctrine of the Faith's declaration *Dominus Jesus* (2000), were also visible. Ever more clearly, the fundamental issue has turned out to be that we are not in agreement about how the full unity that we seek is to be understood and where the ecumenical path is supposed to lead.[2]

A new stimulus and a new vision were necessary. Pope Francis gave them in his totally personal way. He is a man of encounter. Therefore, in his speech on November 30, 2014 in the Patriarchal Church St. George in Istanbul, on the occasion of the feast of the patron saint there, the Apostle Andrew, he said,

> Meeting each other, seeing each other face to face, exchanging the embrace of peace, and praying for each other, are all essential aspects of our journey toward the restoration of full communion. All of this precedes and always accompanies that other essential aspect of this journey, namely, theological dialogue. An authentic dialogue is, in every case, an encounter

between persons with a name, a face, a past, and not merely a meeting of ideas.

In addition to words, Pope Francis makes expressive gestures of reconciliation. They have a tradition in ecumenical relations.[3] When Pope Paul VI on December 14, 1975 knelt down in the Sistine Chapel before the Metropolitan Meliton, the envoy of the then Ecumenical Patriarch Demetrios, and asked for forgiveness for past sins against the Orthodox, some members of the Curia did not understand that act. Pope John Paul II also encountered incomprehension and criticism concerning his repeated requests for forgiveness, most noticeably at the celebration of the Eucharist on the first Sunday of Lent in the Jubilee Year 2000. Archbishop Bergoglio had elicited incomprehension and harsh criticism when he allowed evangelical pastors to lay hands on him as a sign of prayer for intercession.[4] Now as pope, during his visit in Istanbul, he bowed before the Ecumenical Patriarch and asked for his blessing. As a consequence, Pope Francis stands in the best tradition of popes who have been criticized by many in curial circles.

There is another fact as well. Pope Francis situates the unity of Christians in its total context and in the service of the unity and peace of humanity. In the Joint Declaration with the Ecumenical Patriarch, he expressed their common concern "for the current situation in Iraq, Syria and the whole Middle East. We are united in the desire for peace and stability and in the will to promote the resolution of conflicts through dialogue and reconciliation." In his address in the Patriarchal Church, he said, "In today's world, voices are being raised that we cannot ignore and that implore our Churches to live deeply our identity as disciples of the Lord Jesus Christ." He mentions the voice of the poor, the voices of the victims of conflicts, and the voices of young people who live without hope, overcome by mistrust and resignation.

New theological stimuli are also not lacking. It has already become clear that making the gospel the starting point and emphasizing the fundamental significance of the gospel, Holy Scripture, and preaching goes far in meeting Protestant concerns and the theology of the Reformers. *Communio* ecclesiology, emphasis upon the significance of local churches, resistance to a monolithic understanding of the church and his self-description as Bishop of Rome, emphasis upon the synodal principle, and willingness to engage in dialogue about the exercise of primacy—all of that corresponds to important concerns of the churches of the East.

Surprising talk of a "conversion" of the papacy (*EG* 32) brings to mind the significant ecumenical memorandum of the group from Dombes, *Pour la conversion des Églises* (For the conversion of the churches, 1991). It is thereby clear from the outset that ecumenism is not something like a summons and invitation to other Christians to return to the bosom of the Catholic Church, but only expressed in somewhat friendlier terms than previously. Evangelization presupposes the church's self-evangelization and the unity of the church presupposes its own conversion.

Pope Francis caused a theological stir by adopting the position of "unity through diversity" proposed by Lutheran theologian Oscar Cullman (1902–1999), who was very close to Paul VI and was an observer at the Council.[5] Already Joseph Ratzinger had spoken positively about this concept. On this point too, affinities with the early Tübingen tradition are striking.[6] In this way a fundamental concern has been addressed, which, in the Lutheran World Federation, has become the leading ecumenical perspective under the title "Unity in Reconciled Diversity."[7] In another way, this model is fundamental in dialogues with the Orthodox churches: the trinitarian perspective of the unity of God in the threeness of hypostases (persons).[8]

The formula of unity through diversity can be understood differently according to the respective underlying Catholic, Orthodox, or Lutheran ecclesiology and, correspondingly, it is also expounded differently. With this formula, Pope Francis means more than mutual recognition of the existing churches. He proceeds from the principle that the whole is placed over the part and, therefore, it is not only the sum of the parts or their combination (*EG* 234–37). In this way he gives a great deal of room to the diversity and the individual character of the different churches. His model of unity is not that of a sphere "where every point is equidistant from the center, and there are no differences between them. Instead, it is the polyhedron [that is, three-dimensional body with many angles and surfaces], which reflects the convergence of all its parts, each of which preserves its distinctiveness" and seeks "to gather in this polyhedron the best of each" (*EG* 236).[9]

If we are talking about a precious stone, the polyhedron has its own beauty and, as a prism, it breaks up the light falling upon it in a multifarious, wonderfully beautiful way. Of course, for starters that is an image that has to be translated into a concept and then into concrete ecumenical practice. Nevertheless, it is worthwhile to think about the precise significance of this original and stimulating image. It replaces the model of concentric circles, often used on the Catholic side, and it makes possible a unity that preserves the distinctiveness of the different churches without, however, obscuring the identity of the whole. This image enables a mutual, ecumenical process of learning and a complementary relationship that is mutually enriching (*EG* 246). That is harmony, as created by the Spirit of God.

If this conception of unity is already surprising, then it is equally surprising that Pope Francis makes use of it in reference not only to the Orthodox churches and the traditional Lutheran and Reformed churches, but also applies it to the evangelical and

Pentecostal churches. That is a new and a heretofore scarcely imaginable step forward. Francis has already moved in this direction with his video message on January 14, 2014 to a conference of Pentecostal leaders in the United States. He has fully taken this step with his impressive speech during the meeting in Caserta on July 28, 2014. That has elicited a great resonance—among some, understandably, a cautious to critical reservation, but among very many Pentecostal Christians, excitement.

In light of the rapidly growing spread of Pentecostal churches —one estimates about six hundred million believers worldwide by now—the significance of this step cannot be so easily overestimated. Up to now, on the local level there was, to be sure, some human and Christian contact. But, on the whole, the climate among Pentecostal churches was very often decidedly anti-Catholic; and on the Catholic side, it was hardly less critical and injurious. The Pentecostal churches—as the pope himself admitted and for which he apologized—have been described as fanatics and, so to speak, as crazies. Francis refers to the persecution of Pentecostal Christians during the era of Italian fascism and asks for forgiveness for those Catholics who participated in it. For the pope, Pentecostal Christians are brothers whom we have rediscovered, like Jacob's sons rediscovered their brother Joseph in Egypt.

The pope is realistic; he speaks of the path that we have to travel together. To bishops from the Southern Hemisphere, when they came to Rome for their *ad limina* visits and complained about the difficulties and challenges caused by the proselytism of the Pentecostal churches, I was accustomed to say that we should not talk about what we judge to be wrong with the Pentecostal churches, but should above all ask ourselves what is wrong with us that our own faithful run away from us. Even if we cannot adopt everything that concerns the style or the content of the Pentecostal movement, we can nonetheless learn many things from them about how one can address and attract people with evangelization.

No one who looks at the situation realistically and soberly will have any illusions that the journey to realizing unity will not be long and difficult. The pope himself is realistic enough when he speaks of fraternity and friendship, which—in view of the situation—is already quite a bit and would be an important Christian witness to the outside world. In general, taking a deep breath is necessary. Anyway, Pope Francis concludes his video message with the remarkable sentence, "The mystery of unity has already begun."

Unity has really begun today in the "ecumenism" of the blood of martyrs, who come from all churches. Already Pope John Paul II, out of his experience of the twentieth century, spoke poignantly of the ecumenism of martyrs and, in the Jubilee Year 2000 in the presence of representatives from all of the churches, he held a large ecumenical service at the Colosseum in Rome.[10] Pope Francis takes up that topic with a view to the martyrs of the twenty-first century. In his address to members of the Catholic Fraternity of Charismatic Covenant Communities and Fellowships, he spoke of spiritual ecumenism on October 31, 2014,

> praying and proclaiming together that Jesus is Lord, and coming together to help the poor in all their poverty. This must be done while never forgetting in our day that the blood of Jesus, poured out by many Christian martyrs in various parts of the world, calls us and compels us towards the goal of unity. For persecutors, we are not divided, we are not Lutherans, Orthodox, Evangelicals, Catholics…No! We are one in their eyes! For persecutors we are Christians! They are not interested in anything else. This is the ecumenism of blood that we experience today.

This ecumenism of blood must give Christians a new impetus. It recalls what Tertullian said: "The blood of martyrs is the seed of new Christians."[11]

The pope knows that the path to unity requires staying power for the long haul. We touch thereby upon a final point, which is important for Pope Francis. At the ecumenical celebration in the Church of the Holy Sepulchre in Jerusalem on May 25, 2014, on the occasion of the fiftieth anniversary of the meeting between Pope Paul VI and Patriarch Athenagoras, he said,

> Clearly we cannot deny the divisions which continue to exist among us, the disciples of Jesus: this sacred place makes us even more painfully aware of how tragic they are. And yet, fifty years after the embrace of those two venerable Fathers, we realize with gratitude and renewed amazement how it was possible, at the prompting of the Holy Spirit, to take truly significant steps towards unity. We know that much distance still needs to be travelled before we attain that fullness of communion which can also be expressed by sharing the same Eucharistic meal, something we ardently desire; yet our disagreements must not frighten us and paralyze our progress. We need to believe that, just as the stone before the tomb was cast aside, so too every obstacle to our full communion will also be removed. This will be a grace of resurrection, of which we can have a foretaste even today.

The pope repeatedly refers to the biblical message of patience, perseverance, standing firm under burdens (*hypomone*), and the ability to wait until the time of the harvest (*EG* 24, 44, 105, 146, 165, 171–72, 222). For him, the principle that time has priority over space is true (*EG* 222–25). He does not want to get short-term results. He does not want to occupy positions, but wants to put processes into motion and create a dynamic that will bear fruit at the right time.

That does not mean that ecumenism is deferred until the day the cows come home. The fruits of ecumenical efforts become apparent not only in a mountain of innumerable documents expressing increasing agreement. They are evident, above all, in the growing friendship and collaboration between the churches on all levels—on the level of parishes, dioceses, and communities, as well as on the international level and in the relationships of the Holy See. First and foremost, Pope Francis is concerned about this ecumenism of friendship. Here is where his special, personal charisma lies. He is convinced that ecumenical friendship is necessary as the indispensable presupposition and accompaniment of theological ecumenism and that it will bear fruit for full unity, how and when Jesus Christ intends. Even if we have not yet achieved the full unity of the church, Christianity's unity and collaboration is already clearly taking shape.

IX

NEW FEATURES IN INTERRELIGIOUS DIALOGUE

What is true of ecumenical dialogue is true in a different way of dialogue with Judaism and with other religions and cultures. In this context, we cannot go into details; a few points will have to suffice.[1] The fundamental points of view are prescribed by the Second Vatican Council and were further developed and enlarged upon since then in many declarations of episcopal conferences and the Holy See.[2] The church confesses Christ as the light of the peoples and it understands itself as "a sacrament, that is, a sign and instrument both of a very closely knit union with God and of the unity of the whole human race" (LG 1, 9, 48, among others). The Council rejects nothing of what is true and holy in other religions. It recognizes the seeds of truth in other cultures and religions and seeks dialogue and collaboration with them (GS 3; AG 11; NA 1–2).

From the very beginning of his pontificate, Pope Francis took up this concern and put his personal stamp on interreligious dialogue as well as on ecumenical dialogue. For Francis it is not only a matter of dialogue about the common as well as different cultural and religious traditions, but also about a common contribution to the well-being of the poor, the weak, and the suffering;

it is about common service to justice, reconciliation, and peace as it is about "keeping alive in the world the thirst for the Absolute." In this work he also feels himself close to those human beings who admittedly profess no religious tradition, but who nonetheless are in search of the true, the good, and the beautiful—which God is— and whom he regards as allies in the defense of human dignity, the establishment of peaceful coexistence among peoples, and the attentive preservation of creation.[3] In principle, brotherliness is for him the foundation and the path of peace in the world.[4]

These concerns received expression in meeting with the Jewish people, who are especially dear to Pope Francis, and in the prayer meeting for peace at the Vatican, to which the president of Israel and the president of the Palestinian Territories came on June 8, 2014, in response to his invitation.[5] In a still larger context, there is the declaration against human trafficking and modern slavery, a declaration that was initiated by the pope and then signed in the Vatican on December 2, 2014, together with representatives of other religions and churches. In it, the religious leaders also condemned forced labor, forced prostitution, and trafficking in human organs. The signatories committed themselves to mobilizing the faithful and "people of good will."

Mutual respect and esteem, the recognition of human dignity and human rights—especially freedom of religion—as well as the rejection of religious fundamentalism and terrorism in the name of religion defined the dialogue with Muslims during the pope's visit to Ankara and Istanbul from November 28 to 30, 2014. The pope made a case for joint efforts for a peace process in the Near and Middle East, which has been plagued with ongoing, fatal conflicts. In this way, the pope moved onto the ground of that section of the Council's Declaration on the Church's Relationship to Non-Christian Religions that pertains to Muslims. In addition, he took his place in the tradition of then apostolic delegate to Turkey, Angelo Roncalli, the later John XXIII, as well as in the tradition of Popes Paul VI, John Paul II, and Benedict XVI, in whose footsteps Pope Francis has undertaken his trip to the Holy Land as well as his trip to Turkey.

The focus of Francis' pontificate shall be Asia, the continent with its ancient cultures, to which an ever-greater significance is due in keeping with its growing, worldwide influence. During his visit in Korea, in his meeting with the bishops of Asia, the pope already clearly addressed this dialogue with Asia and the relation of dialogue and Catholic identity.[6] On a number of occasions, especially during the beatification of the Korean martyrs, he referred to the many contemporary martyrs in Asia.[7] With the exception of the Philippines and, to a certain extent, Korea, Christians are still a minority in Asia. After the Korea trip in August 2014, the trip to Sri Lanka and the Philippines in January 2015 certainly emphasized further aspects of the pope's focus on Asia. Rumor has it that, in a different context, beatification is being considered for the important missionary to China, Matteo Ricci, who already in the sixteenth and seventeenth centuries strove successfully to enculturate Christianity in Chinese culture, but was met with hostility from short-sighted individuals and was stopped. If he had been listened to, the history of the church in China would have turned out differently. Let us hope that in the near future there, the door will again be opened wider for the gospel.

X

A POOR CHURCH
FOR THE POOR

Pope Francis' desire for reform and renewal extends beyond the usual intraecclesial and ecumenical matters. Already in his first meeting with representatives of the media, he made clear the explosive nature of his program as he explained the motives that led him to choose the name Francis, and he added, "Oh, how I would like a poor church for the poor!"[1] Accordingly, the name *Francis* stands for the policy of being a poor church for the poor. The pope has repeatedly expressed his vision; in *Evangelii gaudium* (53–60, 197–291, among others) he has again explained it in detail.[2]

This program has attracted a lot of attention, but has also raised critical questions. The question is, can a poor church simultaneously be a church for the poor? Doesn't the church need means in order to be able to help the poor? In order to be able to help, isn't it dependent upon hospitals, schools, retirement homes, and other institutions? And doesn't the church itself need worldly means in order to be able to exercise her service? It would be naive to want to contest all of that.[3]

The question, therefore, is not whether the church shall possess any kind of worldly goods, but rather how and, above all, for what purpose shall the church use the goods entrusted to it.

Does the church use them for the poor or chiefly for its own safeguarding and its own interests? Is there transparency about its use of money and goods, and are decisions about them made according to transparent procedures? With the reform of Vatican finance, Francis has in the meantime led the way with a good example, which must be followed by many other steps in Rome as well as in local churches. Admittedly, the basic problem still has not thereby been touched.

Pope Francis' option for a poor church is ultimately grounded christologically (*EG* 198, 232).[4] Jesus has come to proclaim the good news to the poor (Luke 4:18). The first beatitude of the Sermon on the Mount reads, "Blessed are the poor in spirit, for theirs is the kingdom of heaven" (Matt 5:3; cf. Luke 6:20). In saying this, Jesus does not despise prosperity nor does he idealize poverty. Prosperity can also be understood, in the Old Testament sense, as a blessing from God. Jesus, however, knows about the dangers of wealth. Wealth can give a false sense of security and can smother the seed of the kingdom of God (Matt 13:22). Being poor in spirit means not placing one's hope in earthly riches, but placing it only in God. Voluntary poverty, therefore, is a prophetic sign of the coming reign of God.

Jesus himself has given an example of this sign. In one of the oldest texts in the New Testament, in the pre-Pauline hymn in the Letter to the Philippians, it is said of Jesus,

> Who, though he was in the form of God...
> emptied himself,
>   taking the form of a slave,
> being born in human likeness. (Phil 2:6–7)

Paul took up this motif: "Though he was rich, yet for your sakes he became poor, so that by his poverty you might become rich" (2 Cor 8:9). The church, therefore, in following Jesus as his disciples, must itself be poor so that it can make others rich.

In the original Jerusalem community, they all held everything in common (Acts 2:44). "The poor" was the self-description of the original community in Jerusalem (Rom 15:26; Gal 2:10). This model repeatedly played a role in the history of the church. Ancient monasticism was oriented to this model and consequently introduced a poverty movement that continues to this very day. In the Middle Ages, there were, time and again, counter movements to a powerful and rich church. The best known movement and one that has been fruitful down to today is the poverty movement unleashed by Francis of Assisi.

The theme of a poor church also played a role at the Second Vatican Council. In an address in preparation for the Council on September 11, 1962, already John XXIII had spoken of a church of the poor. In the documents of the Council, this concern did not become a dominant theme; however, it was not entirely lacking. The fundamental text is found in the Constitution on the Church: "Just as Christ carried out the work of redemption in poverty and persecution, so the Church is called to follow the same route.... Thus, the Church...is not set up to seek earthly glory, but to proclaim, even by its own example, humility and self-sacrifice"; thus "the Church encompasses with love all who are afflicted with human suffering and in the poor and afflicted sees the image of its poor and suffering Founder. It does all it can to relieve their need and in them it strives to serve Christ" (*LG* 8:3). Best known is the statement of the Pastoral Constitution: the church shares "the joys and the hopes, the griefs and the anxieties of the men of this age, especially those who are poor or in any way afflicted" (*GS* 1).[5]

In this spirit, shortly before the end of the Council, on November 16, 1965 in the catacombs of Domitilla in Rome, forty bishops forged the so-called Catacomb Pact "For a Servant and

Poor Church," which five hundred additional bishops subsequently joined. They committed themselves to a series of voluntary obligations concerning lifestyle, vestments, titles, and engagement on behalf of the poor.[6] Among the first to sign were bishops such as Hélder Câmara and Aloísio Lorscheider and Auxiliary Bishop Julius Angerhausen from Essen, Germany. After the Council, Archbishop Óscar Romero of San Salvador is to be mentioned. On March 14, 1980, he was gunned down during the celebration of the Mass by a soldier commissioned for the task because Romero, in the spirit of Catholic social teaching, had campaigned for the rights of campesinos.[7] In many Roman circles, he was viewed suspiciously. Pope Francis now has put into motion again the process of beatification, which had been blocked. The beatification of this upright witness to truth and justice would be an important and conspicuous sign. .

After the Council, the topic of liberation theology was taken up. The second plenary assembly of the Latin American episcopate formulated the option for the poor in 1968 in Medellín; the assembly in Puebla in 1979 spoke of the preferential option for the poor; and the seventh general assembly in Aparecida in 2007 repeated this option, grounded it christologically, and expanded it through an option for the excluded.[8] The architect of the document from Aparecida was Cardinal Jorge Bergoglio as chair of the editorial committee. Therefore, it is hardly surprising that Aparecida is cited in many places in *Evangelii gaudium*.[9] The preferential option for the poor did not remain a Latin American anomaly. John Paul II and Pope Benedict XVI adopted it in their own teaching pronouncements.[10] In his opening speech in Aparecida, Benedict XVI grounded the preferential option christologically. In his address at the conclusion of his visit to Germany, on September 25, 2011 in Freiburg, under the heading "Becoming Unworldly," Benedict basically addressed nothing other than what

Francis is saying today. At that time, to a considerable extent people did not understand him or they did not want to understand him.[11] Now Francis shows clearly, in a programmatic way, what the issue is, not only through his words, but also through his own simple and plain lifestyle, the way he appears on the public stage, and through his gestures.

With the preferential option for the poor and a poor church, Pope Francis stands in the line of a long tradition. He can rightly say that the entire tradition gives witness to the option for the poor (EG 198). In this way, he takes up an often neglected concern of the Council and introduces a new phase of conciliar reception. To date the church was concerned more with internal renovation, the reform of the liturgy and structural reform; now the church shall go out to the outskirts of its own territory and into new sociocultural surroundings (EG 30).

The program that Pope Francis is laying out sounds like anything but a gospel of joy that is cheaply and superficially understood. With strong words, he castigates spiritual worldliness, especially of the clergy, which relies on possessions, influence, privileges, or on organization, planning, doctrinal and disciplinary security, authoritarian elite consciousness, or a socially glamorous lifestyle. Such spiritual worldliness is for Pope Francis the worst temptation that can threaten the church (EG 93–97, 207). Those are hefty and provocative theses, which are painful and incite opposition. But the gospel that Jesus proclaimed was also not harmless.

The challenge touches each individual. It pertains to the lifestyle of the upper as well as the lower clergy; it applies equally to the lifestyle of laypeople in church service. It pertains also to religious congregations. Admittedly, they have taken the vow of poverty in the sense of giving up individual worldly goods at their personal disposal; but in general—and not only in Germany—

they are institutionally ensured by their religious community by no means to a lesser degree than most secular Christians for their daily keep, for cases of illness, and for their care in old age.[12] What is required of everyone is simplicity, plainness, and frugality in one's personal lifestyle, as in institutional self-presentation.

One may dismiss these inquiries about the lifestyle of the church, its representatives, and its members as unrealistic or one may perceive them even as unpleasant, indeed as unfair and offensive. Some of these inquiries may in fact arise from a self-righteous or even malicious obsession with scandals, with which people want to make a name for themselves in public. As Christians who appeal to the gospel, we must nonetheless face the questions honestly.

Such questions about the church—about both large churches in Germany—are not new. Already two great ecumenical witnesses of the last century, Dietrich Bonhoeffer and Alfred Delp, clearly foresaw the necessity of departing from a rich and powerful church.[13] They have been much quoted, but in this matter little listened to. The joint synod of the German dioceses (1971–1975) attempted with renewed insistence to bring back awareness of the problem of poverty.[14] But even then Karl Rahner had to lament the church's unreadiness for poverty.[15]

With his program of a poor church for the poor, Pope Francis directs a serious inquiry at the church. The challenge pertains to the church as an institution, its self-presentation, and the way it deals with money and goods. The challenge is directed primarily at affluent churches in an affluent society, like the church in Germany.[16] True, there are attempts also in the poor churches to reactivate feudal structures, which in the meantime we have largely overcome. Nonetheless, the church is not supposed to depend on political and social influence and glamor; it is not to rely only on programs, planning, and organizations, but rather to rely on spiritual radiance.

Pope Francis is convinced that we can only overcome the *acedia*, the crippling force that pulls us down, and can direct our attention upward and regain our spiritual momentum if we, as a poor church for the poor, reclaim the joy and spark of the gospel and set our hope on God and his providence. Great saints like John Don Bosco and Mother Teresa have shown the way. That is no liberal program; that is a radical and very challenging program of reform and renewal, in the sense of poverty in the face of God (Matt 5:3) and in the face of human beings. Pope Francis is convinced that we can learn precisely this joy from the poor (EG 198).

XI

THE CHALLENGE OF POVERTY IN TODAY'S WORLD

I n today's world, the church encounters many diverse challenges: the challenge of peace; the forced migration of people fleeing persecution or extreme poverty; the challenge of intercultural and interreligious dialogue; the preservation of creation; the protection of life; the crisis of the family; scientific and technological progress; the increase in knowledge and information and the simultaneous loss of orientation, with a concomitant change in culture, which is often described as a shift in values; and the challenge of secularization and relativism (*EG* 52, 64). Among these multiple challenges, Pope Francis' attention in *Evangelii gaudium* is directed primarily toward the social challenges, especially the problem of the poor and the problem of poverty (*EG* 52, 60–67, all of chapter 4). For Pope Francis this is one of the key problems today, if not *the* key problem underlying many others.[1]

In the background is the appalling scandal of poverty and misery, especially in the Southern Hemisphere, from which the pope himself comes and whose conflicts he has personally experienced. He does not overlook the positive consequences of globalization; however, from the perspective of the periphery, he sees more clearly than we Europeans usually do its devastating consequences for millions of people. That explains why he often adduces extreme examples that defy generalization, but which unsparingly expose the global situation and, therefore, cannot also be easily pushed aside. For the pope it is a matter of a prophetic outcry and issuing a clarion call in view of millions of human beings, who are still regarded only as problem cases, as "trash" and "garbage" (*EG* 53). The pope wants to raise his voice against the globalization of indifference in the face of this situation (*EG* 54). He calls us to hear the cry of the poor (*EG* 187). In the process, he does not shy away from using harsh words in prophetic language—very clearly once again in his speech on October 28, 2014 in the Vatican before participants in the "World Meeting of Popular Movements" (*Movimentos populares*).

Understandably, these statements have found special interest in the secular media, but also in some cases sharp criticism.[2] In doing this, some have not always paid attention to the fact that the pope did not want to present in *Evangelii gaudium* a document about social matters or an economic analysis (*EG* 15, 184). The latter is not the task nor is it within the competency of a pope. The pope's program of a poor church for the poor is, first of all, an ecclesial, pastoral, and spiritual program. According to its literary genre, it is an *exhortatio*, an exhortation that wants to stir up and embolden. It is directed toward faithful Christians in order to invite them to a new stage of evangelization (*EG* 1) and, in this context, it directs their attention toward the challenges that today's world poses for evangelization.

Pope Francis proceeds according to his familiar method of spiritual discernment on the basis of the gospel (*EG* 50–51). He wants to uncover misguided attitudes, which lead to a misguided economy. For him, the economy is a communicative occurrence of the exchange of goods between human beings; therefore, massive poverty is not simply a natural fate, but rather the result of a perverted economy, which regards and uses the human person only as an individual and, because of such individualism, destroys the social bonds, especially the bond of families (*EG* 67).

The social crisis, therefore, is an anthropological crisis, in which no longer the human person, but rather money stands at the center and has become the idol that determines everything. To it corresponds an unbridled consumerism, which reduces the human being to a *homo oeconomicus*, the one who produces and consumes (*EG* 60, 63, 67). The pope directs a fourfold no against this consumerism: no to an economy of exclusion, in which people are pushed to the margins and are discarded; no to the idolatry of money and the ideology of the absolute autonomy of the markets; no to money, which rules rather than serves; no to social inequality, which incites violence (*EG* 53–60).

Only in this total context are his statements critical of the market understandable, statements that have been especially criticized. Above all, the statement, "This economy kills" has led to opposition. However, one has to read that sentence precisely. It doesn't say "The economy kills," but "*This* economy;" that is, a particular kind of economy kills. These statements are to be understood as criticism of the negative outgrowths of the capitalist system, which are found in many countries of the world. However, they point beyond that to a fundamental flaw in the system.

Pope Francis is, above all, critical of the trickle-down theory, which proceeds from the belief that economic progress over time leaks and trickles down to the poor as well (*EG* 54).[3] This theory ultimately can be traced back to the founder of classical political economy, Adam Smith (1723–1790). During the era of the Reagan administration[4], this theory had a politically elevated status, which led to a wide-ranging deregulation of markets. This theory is much debated among experts. Its supporters concede that, in fact, very many people suffer from extreme poverty, but they say that this situation has demonstrably been improved through global economic programs. In support, they refer to the United Nations' 2013 Report on the World Economy. The numbers cannot be contested. Nevertheless, neither is the factual problem of the misery of so many human beings thereby resolved, nor the fundamental problem of an economic system that causes such misery.

Francis quotes the papal social encyclicals[5] and the Compendium of the Church's Social Teaching[6] very often. Proceeding from the spirit of Catholic social teaching, the pope is concerned with more than alms and individual assistance, with more than the church's help organizations and help programs, as beneficial as they are in individual cases (EG 202). All Christians, their pastors included, must be concerned about a better configuration of the world (EG 183), the structural causes of poverty (EG 202), a holistic fostering of human welfare (EG 181–82), and a holistic development of the poor (EG 188, 203). Structural changes and engagement on behalf of a more just social order are necessary (EG 202–7, 217–21). With all of that said, the mission of the church is "not a humanitarian activity. It is not a show where we count how many people come as a result of our publicity; it is something much deeper, which escapes all measurement" (EG 279). This holistic approach is usually overlooked in the criticism of the pope's critique.

The church's social teaching proceeds from the fact that the goods of the world belong to all human beings (EG 190, 192). Pope Francis quotes the church father Chrysostom: "Not to share one's wealth with the poor is to steal from them and to take away their livelihood" (EG 57). All should have a share in the Earth and its goods; all have a right to lodging and also a right to work, through which they are able to collaborate and share in the social process and its progress. Work befits the dignity of the human person. Through their work, human beings are supposed to be not simply passive recipients and thereby objects, but rather active cocreators and thereby subjects of the economic process.[7] The poor have something to contribute to that process; indeed, we have much to learn from them (*EG* 198). The work, or rather the unemployment especially of so many young people in many countries of Europe and the world, represents for the pope a key problem. He has made that clear once again in the already mentioned speech at the international conference of *Movimentos populares*.

In addition to the principle of subsidiarity, which is grounded in the dignity of every individual human being, comes the principle of the solidarity of all people. From this perspective, Pope Francis addresses a second contemporary key problem: migration, flight, and the reception of refugees. Hospitality toward strangers, the needy, and the persecuted is a fundamental obligation already in the Old and the New Testament; hostility toward strangers, on the other hand, can and should not exist among Christians (Gen 18:1–15; Isa 58:7; Wisd 19:13–17; Matt 25:35; Rom 12:13; Heb 13:2).[8] Pope Pius XII described the reception of refugees, in fact, as their human right.[9] In the last few decades, these statements have been diplomatically weakened. Now Pope Francis has retrieved prophetic language and has chosen thereby very strong and clear words, which have encountered opposition. Nonetheless, in the language of the Bible, the pope asks, "Who is your brother?" (Gen 4:9; *EG* 210–11).[10]

It is significant that the pope undertook his very first trip on July 8, 2013 to Lampedusa, where the drama and misery of refugees and the failure of the European community was public. There he sharply criticized the lack of solidarity and globalized indifference. During his visit to the Roman center for refugees *Astalli* on September 10, 2013, he said, "Solidarity, this word that frightens the developed world. People try to avoid saying it. Solidarity to them is almost a bad word. But it is our word!" In this context, he also emphasized that refugees are not simply a problem, but that they can contribute something to our culture. The church belongs on the side of the weak. The reception of the poor and the promotion of justice is entrusted not only to specialists, but must catch the attention of our total pastoral ministry.

With all of this, Pope Francis is not a fundamental opponent of the market. His criticism of capitalism pertains to the absolute autonomy of markets and financial speculation (EG 56) and, as in the case of John Paul II, is directed against an unbridled, ideological global capitalism, in which free enterprise is not integrated into social legislation and everything becomes dependent upon the commercial interests of capital, which leads to the economic quantification of all spheres of life (Cardinal Reinhard Marx). The economic system to be distinguished from it is what we call a social market economy. It takes seriously the role of the business owner, the market, private property, and the creativity of the human person, but places them within the parameters of a social order and at the service of human freedom and the body politic.[11] It is necessary to respect not only human rights as the rights of individuals, but also the rights of peoples, especially poor people, for the Earth belongs to all (EG 190).

Pope Francis carries the church's social teaching forward along the lines marked out by Pope Benedict XVI. Whereas the church's classical social teaching proceeds from the idea of justice, Pope Benedict and now Pope Francis go a step further. Benedict has not replaced, but deepened its grounding in justice by giving it a foundation in love (charity). Love does not annul justice; love presupposes it and surpasses it. Justice is the minimum; love, the maximum of social obligation.[12] In this sense, love is "the principle not only of micro-relationships (with friends, with family members or within small groups) but also of macro-relationships (social, economic and political ones)."[13]

At this point, Pope Francis commences with the message of mercy. That does not mean that for him justice has been played out; he speaks of justice in very many places.[14] He wants to emphasize the social dimension of the gospel, whose core is love (*EG* 176–79, 193–94) "For this reason, the service of charity is also a constituent element of the Church's mission....To the extent that God reigns within us, the life of society will be a setting for universal fraternity, justice, peace and dignity" (*EG* 179–80). Authentic faith always includes the deep wish to change the world, transmit values, and leave behind something better after our earthly pilgrimage (*EG* 183). Without such a commitment, religious practices are barren, empty, hypocritical talk (*EG* 207).

By saying this, Francis does not wish to propound a concrete economic program. He is concerned with the anthropological crisis, in which money has become mammon and an idol (*EG* 55). He is demanding a new culture of life and a new lifestyle, which is defined not by having, but by giving and sharing (*EG* 57). At the same time, he demands a culture that decides about what is truly necessary, that preserves from distraction and again frees our sight anew for what is essential and for God. Above all, solidarity with the poor directly affects our relationship to God (*EG* 196–97).

The holistic, social-ethics approach of the pope is misunderstood by some pro-life individuals. They opine that the pope does not fight hard enough for the protection of the life of unborn children.[15] Certainly such a commitment is commendable, especially in the present situation. The protection of life, however, pertains not only to the beginning and the end of life, as important as both of them obviously are. The protection of life pertains to the entire course of life from conception to natural death; it encompasses engagement on behalf of those born and thus for social justice; it includes humane care of poor, sick, and suffering human beings. Therefore, one may not restrict the church's moral teaching to only a few facets of life, as important and fundamental as they also are (*EG* 39).

A new culture of life includes a new attitude toward creation and gives rise to the ecological question.[16] Already in Pope Benedict we find approaches to a theological reflection about ecological questions.[17] In his homily upon the occasion of his installation on March 19, 2013, Francis referred to Saint Joseph as *Custos*, as protector. The pope spoke of affection in relation to creation. In this regard, Francis of Assisi is an exemplar for him.[18] In *Evangelii gaudium*, he writes, "We love this magnificent planet on which God has put us, and we love the human family which dwells here" (*EG* 183; cf. 190). Human beings are supposed to be the protectors of creation (*EG* 215). But what have we made of the Earth? An advancing desertification of the soil, the deforestation of the forests, the pollution of bodies of water, the devastation of the environment, and destruction through wars....Therefore, the pope is planning an encyclical on questions of ecology. Like Francis of Assisi in the Canticle of the Sun, Francis is concerned about the rediscovery of beauty as a path to God.[19]

XII

EUROPE—WHERE ARE
YOUR IDEALS?

All of the challenges mentioned pertain also to us Europeans;
they concern the church and the peoples of Europe. The history of Christianity is tightly bound up with the history of Europe,
and European history is bound up with Rome and the bishop of
Rome. The idea of Rome was present already in the ancient world
and then in the entire history of Europe as the idea of unity or as
an anti-Roman feeling that Europe had to work away at.[1] Pope
Francis' immediate predecessors were all genuine Europeans, for
whom the unity of Europe, the European legacy, and the continuing mandate growing out of it were close to their hearts.[2]

As bishop of Rome, Pope Francis neither can nor wants to
evade his European responsibility. But his angle of vision is different. He comes from the other side of the world and he views
Europe from the periphery. In consistent fashion, as bishop of
Rome he traveled first to Lampedusa, then to the poorest region
of Italy, to Sardinia, and to the poorest country in Europe, to Albania. He sees many things from the periphery more clearly and dis-
tinctly than we Europeans, who somehow still believe that we are
at the center of world events. From the periphery, Pope Francis
sees Europe's crisis. During his visit to the Sant'Egidio community

on June 15, 2014, he said, "Europe has grown tired; we must help it to become young again and to rediscover its roots." In this way, he recalls the spirit of the European project of the founding fathers of Europe and the desire to create a common space in which human beings and peoples can live and live together.

Pope Francis also gave voice to his impression of a tired Europe during his visit to the European Parliament and the Council of Europe on November 25, 2014, in Strasbourg. Since the visit of John Paul II to the European Parliament a quarter century ago in 1988, the world situation has changed fundamentally. At that time, the Berlin Wall was still standing and Europe was divided in two by the Iron Curtain. Since then, the world has become more complex and confusing.

> A world, increasingly interconnected and global…
> has, as a consequence, become less and less "Eurocen-
> tric." Despite a larger and more influential Union,
> Europe seems to give the impression of being some-
> what elderly and haggard, feeling less and less a pro-
> tagonist in a world which frequently regards it with
> aloofness, mistrust and even, at times, suspicion.[3]

Pope Francis is also fully aware of Europe's great legacy. It is the idea of the transcendent dignity of the human being as a person, as it was developed upon the foundation of the Greeks and Romans in the history of Christianity.[4] Pope Francis does not thereby, like his predecessors, stress the church's contribution and its continuing mission of preserving this heritage. He speaks conspicuously little of the church, but all the more of service on behalf of human well-being. He speaks of human rights, with the recognition of which the church has toiled so long. He says that one ought not understand human rights only as individual rights, but must understand them in the context of the common good. He mentions the two fundamental concepts of Christian social teaching, subsidiarity and solidarity.

The pope tries to elucidate the religious dimension with two images. He refers to the dispute between Plato and Aristotle, depicted in Raphael's fresco in the Vatican, *The School of Athens*: "Plato's finger is pointed upward, to the world of ideas....Aristotle stretches his hand out before him, towards the viewer, towards Earth, concrete reality."[5] The second image derives from the poem *Il pioppo* (The poplar) of the Italian poet Clemente Rebora (1885–1957). It describes a poplar, which strives upward and is simultaneously rooted in the Earth.[6] For the pope, both images point to the fact that underlining the religious dimension of human beings does not stand in opposition to the legitimate secular character of culture and the state. He knows that the time is past when the church was society's only point of reference for culture. A new kind of Christian presence is needed.[7]

In order to clarify this new kind of Christian presence, Pope Francis draws on his process-oriented approach. The blueprint for lasting peace, which the founding fathers of Europe sought, must be realized in ever-new efforts to awaken peace and to bring peace about. To achieve the good of peace, one may not proceed from a blueprint that excludes those who think or live differently, but must work toward a blueprint for peace that seeks to include them.

The pope names two fundamental challenges of plurality to this aim: "The challenge of *multipolarity* and the challenge of *transversality*."[8] With the concept of multipolarity, he pleads for a Europe of unity in diversity, which excludes hegemonic supremacy and respects the cultural diversity of peoples and of religions. Again he harks back to the image of the polyhedron, in which the unity of the whole preserves the distinctiveness of the different parts. *Transversal communication* means an open, respectful, and enriching exchange between the generations, between people and groups of disparate ancestry and different ethnic, linguistic, and religious traditions in a spirit of mutual understanding and mutual respect.

In this transversal communication, Christianity today can find its place anew. In principle, from the very beginning Europe was characterized by its communicative, dialogical identity, which can also be described as "eccentric identity."[9] In the course of its history, European Christianity assimilated Jewish, Greek-Byzantine, Roman, Celtic, Germanic, Slavic, and Arabic-Islamic elements of culture and transformed itself in a critical and constructive fashion. On this foundation, already Paul VI and then John Paul II thought about the dialogical relation between church and the modern world, which then was near and dear to Benedict XVI, above all, under the heading of faith and reason.[10] Francis takes up these reflections with his idea of transversal global identity and puts them in a new, multipolar, global perspective, in which the church can be an important but no longer the only cultural point of reference and in which Europe must be a global player in a new way with respect not only to global economics, but also intellectual and spiritual matters. Whoever knows how to listen carefully, notes that in this way, not only the end of the old Eurocentric world, but also the end of the Constantinian symbiotic relationship of church and worldly power is being described exactly, without embarking on a path of hostile dualism expressed in secularization and *laicité*.

> This way of thinking also casts light on the contribution which *Christianity* can offer to the cultural and social development of Europe today within the context of a correct relationship between religion and society. In the Christian vision, faith and reason, religion and

society, are called to enlighten one another by mutually supporting one another, and, whenever necessary, purifying one another from the ideological extremes into which they can fall. European society as a whole cannot fail to benefit from a renewed interplay between these two sectors, whether to confront a form of religious fundamentalism which is above all inimical to God, or to remedy a "reductive" rationality which does no honor to humanity.[11]

The pope does not stop with abstract principles. He poses concrete and often downright uncomfortable questions: about the many unemployed young people, about the elderly, all the poor and the weak, and children. Refugees are especially near and dear to him; they are human beings who find in their homeland no possibilities for living, but who—as new Europeans—can also enrich Europe with their talents. Using drastic language, he says that the Mediterranean ought not become a cemetery. Ultimately, he is concerned about the preservation of the natural bases of life, which is incompatible with a throw-away culture and unrestrained consumerism and that demands precisely from Europeans a new lifestyle. Those are uncomfortable words, which clearly identify by name the current challenges.

In view of such tasks, the pope asks Europe, "Where is your vigor? Where is that idealism which inspired and ennobled your history? Where is your spirit of curiosity and enterprise? Where is your thirst for truth, a thirst which hitherto you have passionately shared with the world?"[12]

Pope Francis concluded his visit to the European Parliament with a stirring and emboldening appeal:

The time has come for us to abandon the idea of a Europe which is fearful and self-absorbed, in order to revive and encourage a Europe that is a protagonist and a repository of science, art, music, human values and faith as well. A Europe that contemplates the heavens and pursues lofty ideals. A Europe that cares for, defends, and protects human beings; a Europe that advances surely and securely, a precious point of reference for all humanity![13]

OUTLOOK FOR THE FUTURE:
THE JOY AND THE HOPE
OF THE GOSPEL

The great majority of the people of God and many other people who—in the words of Augustine—are formally outside but in reality are included in the people of God are fascinated to learn how Pope Francis knows how to make the gospel of Jesus Christ present in the church and in the world today. He does that with his kerygmatic and often prophetic speech, with his gestures, and with his thoroughly personal and authentically felt style. In this way, he brings light to the everyday as well as to the big questions of humanity today, questions about the joys and fears, hopes and desires, hardships and distress, guilt and the quest for mercy, upon which all of us are dependent.

Pope Francis is a man of encounter. He has charisma for addressing everyone, the powerful of this world as well as the many small, inconspicuous people about whom nothing is ever written in the newspaper. He conveys his message benevolently, but not tritely; in an inviting but not chummy way; welcoming everyone and virtually embracing everyone and yet shaking them up and often making them uncomfortable. In the process, his speeches are always devoid of agitation; they want to challenge; however, there is absolutely nothing inflammatory and nothing revolutionary about them, understood in the ordinary way. They radiate a deep inner peace, joy, hope, and confidence.

Thus Pope Francis can bear witness to the joy of the gospel for a world that is often joyless and self-constricted. He is convinced that we can only overcome the gravitational pull dragging us down and the paralyzing spiritual inertia that has befallen us through the joy and the lively energy of the gospel. If a house has become dilapidated, beautification measures on the inside do no good. One must first shore up the foundations. Similarly, the church must remember its foundation in the gospel, which was laid once for all and is always present in the Holy Spirit. Returning to evangelical poverty can once again yield spiritual wealth.

Pope Francis proclaims the perpetually valid message of the gospel in its eternal newness and freshness. It doesn't fit into any ready-made template. Francis connects continuity with the great tradition of the church with renewal and ever new surprises. To this also belongs the provocative weightiness of the program of a poor church for the poor. That is not a liberal program; it is a radical program, radical because it goes to the root and is a revolution of tenderness and love. In his speech to the *Movimentos populares*, the pope speaks of a storm of love that alone is capable of transforming the world from within. The revolution of tenderness and love happens, to be sure, with passion, but without force, fanaticism, or anger.

With such a prophetic message, which offers no recipes but rather transmits stimuli, of course questions remain open. They concern the concreteness of the program. Going beyond making appeals, must not the church pursue "concrete" policies, even concrete ecclesial policies? Otherwise, doesn't the church run the risk of being abstract and irrelevant? According to its own self-understanding, the church is indeed a divine and human institution, which includes institutional elements and a wise and forward-looking ecclesial policy. Will Francis, therefore, really trigger a great reform? Or will his pontificate disappoint expectations? These are questions that even many of those who are very fond of Pope Francis are also asking.[1]

Without a doubt, no one can realize a program for the century, such as Pope Francis proposes, within the limited time of one pontificate. That is humanly impossible for one pope. Pope Francis will, to be sure, work step by step on individual points of his program, as he has done up to now. In the process, surprises will not be lacking. The question, however, remains: Will the pope succeed in kicking off a process—such as he has in mind—that will extend beyond this pontificate and no longer be reversible? Or will his pontificate remain only a brief interlude in the church's history?

We humans cannot answer these questions. No one can foresee the future and look at the Holy Spirit's cards. The answer also does not depend on the pope alone. It depends just as much on whether and to what extent his colleagues in the Roman Curia, the local churches, the religious orders, the movements, the associations, the academy and its theological faculties, and many individual Christians seize upon his impulses. One cannot simply lean back in one's easy chair and say, Hang on, let's see what the new pope does. We ourselves must venture out of the starting blocks and set off and sprint. Everyone should understand this statement: "I am a mission on this earth; that is the reason why I am here in this world" (EG 273).

Ultimately, the response to the message of the gospel, which Francis propounds and sets as an example, even in its total weightiness and provocation, can only come from faith. His program for action are the promises in the Beatitudes of the Sermon on the Mount. In faith we know that what is weakness, indeed the gospel's foolishness in the eyes of the world, is its strength

(1 Cor 1:21–25). The path to Easter joy leads over the cross. The power of the pope, therefore, is "the weak power of Christian preaching, not the offer of a Christian ideology," still less "a Christian hegemony" that dictates a faith. The conversion and faith of many individuals "in a community without borders is a reality, which pushes into the depths of history and rattles its surface. And then history is full of surprises."[2] It is a revolution of tenderness and love.

Consequently, the challenge of this pontificate is far more radical than most suspect. It is a challenge for conservatives, who don't want to let themselves be surprised any more by God and who resist reforms, just as it is for progressives, who expect feasible, concrete solutions right here and now. The revolution of tenderness and love and the mysticism of open eyes could disappoint both groups and in the end, nevertheless, receive its due. For the "joy of the gospel" has a promise whose realization never completely comes to fulfillment in history. The church too will always be a church not only of saints, but also of sinners, who time and again are in need of renewal. Nothing is worse than the rage of Cathars, inquisitors, and merciless rigorists, who mourn the loss of a pure church of the past, which never even existed; and nothing is worse than the zeal of enthusiastic, progressive-thinking utopian individuals for a pure and ideal church of the future, which is mercilessly hard on the church's present condition.

Beyond reactionary ideology and fanatical utopia stands the Christian realism of the joy of the gospel. Its eschatological message of hope is realized already now in an emblematic and exemplary fashion in holy men and women who are most inconspicuous. What the pope recommends is the humble path of faithful human beings, who can shift continents and move mountains

(Matt 17:19; 21:21). A little bit of mercy—so he says—can change the world. That is the Christian revolution of revolution, as it is usually understood. It is a revolution in the original sense of the word, the return to the wellspring of the gospel as the way into the future. It is a revolution of mercy.

NOTES

I

1. A first assessment by Jan Heiner Tück, ed., *Der Theologenpapst: Eine kritische Würdigung Benedikts XVI* (Freiburg i. Br.: Herder, 2013); Nicolas Diat, *L'homme qui ne voulait pas être pape: Histoire secrète d'un règne* (Paris: Albin Michel, 2014).

2. Massimo Franco, *C'era una volta un Vaticano* (Milan: Mondadori, 2010); Marco Politi, *Joseph Ratzinger: Crisi di un papato* (Rome: Laterza, 2011).

3. Concerning this deeper dimension of the crisis, see Andrea Riccardi, *Franziskus: Papst der Überraschungen* (Würzburg: Echter, 2014), especially 25–29.

4. A summary, which Cardinal Jaime Ortega published shortly after Francis' election, is in Pope Francis, *"Und jetzt beginnen wir diesen Weg": Die ersten Botschaften des Pontifikats* (Freiburg i. Br.: Herder, 2013), 122–24.

5. Austen Ivereigh's assertion that a certain group of European cardinals had already secured Cardinal Bergoglio's acceptance beforehand in the case he was elected lacks every foundation. *The Great Reformer: Francis and the Making of a Radical Pope* (New York: Henry Holt, 2014), 354–55.

6. Pope Francis, *Und jetzt beginnen wir diesen Weg*, 24.

7. Ibid., 31. Similar comments in his address to the diplomatic corps, ibid., 54–55.

8. The title *bishop of Rome* is one of the oldest titles used for the pope. The title is frequently found in the writings of Gregory the Great, in the Decree of Union of the Council of Florence, in the First Vatican Council, in the Constitution *Lumen gentium* of the Second Vatican Council as well as in the Code of Canon Law of 1917 and in the Code of Canon Law of 1983. The description *sedes apostolica* was also originally applied to the Roman community. See Yves Congar, "Titel, welche für den Papst verwendet werden," *Concilium* (D) 11 (1975): 538–44; here, 538–39.

9. Pope Francis, *Und jetzt beginnen wir diesen Weg*, 15; similarly on the following day in his homily at the celebration of Mass with the cardinals, ibid., 17.

10. Jorge Mario Bergoglio and Abraham Skorka, *On Heaven and Earth*, trans. Alejandro Bermudez and Howard Goodman (New York: Image Books, 2013), 2.

11. Speech during a private visit to an evangelical community in Caserta on July 28, 2014.

12. Only a few of the publications: Sergio Rubin and Francesca Ambrogetti, *Papst Franziskus. Mein Leben—mein Weg: El Jesuita. Die Gespräche mit Jorge Mario Bergoglio* (Freiburg i. Br.: Herder, 2013); Elisabetta Piqué, *Francesco: Vita e rivoluzione* (Turin: Lindau, 2013), expanded English edition: *Pope Francis: Life and Revolution* (Chicago: Loyola, 2014); Andreas N. Bartlogg and Niklaus Kuster, *Franziskus: Der neue Papst und sein Vorbild* (Munich: Hirmer, 2013); Andrea Riccardi, *La Sorpresa di Papa Francesco: Crisi e futuro della Chiesa* (Milan: Mondadori, 2013); Jürgen Erbacher, *Papst Franziskus: Aufbruch und Neuanfang* (Munich: Pattloch, 2013); Pierre Lunel, *Je m'appellerai Francois: Biographie* (Paris: First Editions, 2013); Paul Vallely, *Pope Francis: Untying the Knots* (New York: Bloomsbury, 2013); Luigi Accatoli,

Il vescovo di Roma: Gli esordi di Papa Francesco (Bologna: Edizioni Dehoniane, 2014). Víctor Manuel Fernández in dialogo con Paolo Rodatori, *Il progetto di Francesco: Dove vuole portare la Chiesa* (Bologna: Emi, 2014); Raffaele Luise, *Con le periferie nel cuore* (Milan: Cinisello Balsamo, 2014); Bartolomeo Sorge, *Gesù sorride: Con papa Francesco oltre la religione della paura* (Milan: Piemme, 2014); Giuliano Vicini, *Papa Francesco: La chiesa della misericordia* (Milan: Cinisello Balsamo, 2014); Nello Scavo, *Bergoglios Liste: Papst Franziskus und die argentinische Militärdiktatur* (Freiburg i. Br.: Herder, 2014); Daniel Deckers, *Papst Franziskus: Wider die Trägheit des Herzens. Eine Biographie* (Munich: Beck, 2014); Ivereigh, *The Great Reformer*; Jürgen Erbacher, *Ein radikaler Papst: Die franziskanische Wende* (Munich: Pattloch, 2014), which was published after this manuscript was completed.

13. Giuliano Ferrara, A. Gnocchi, M. Palmero, *Questo papa piace troppo: Un' appassionata lettura critica* (Milan: PIEMME, 2014). Informative and critical comments concerning this criticism: Marco Politi, *Francesco tra i lupi: Il segreto di una rivoluzione* (Rome–Bari: Laterza, 2014).

14. Thus the German book title of the publication from Riccardi, *Franziskus: Papst der Überraschungen*.

II

1. Michael Hesemann, *Das Vermächtnis Benedikts XVI. und die Zukunft der Kirche* (Munich: Herbig, 2013).

2. When asked, he mentions, among others, Josef A. Jungmann, *Die Frohbotschaft und unsere Glaubensverkündigung* (Regensburg: Friedrich Pustet, 1936); Hugo Rahner, *A Theology of Proclamation* (New York: Herder, 1968).

3. On this issue, see the interview of Pope Francis with Antonio Spadaro in *Civiltà cattolica* 164 (2013): 453–57. Also

Spadaro et al., *A Big Heart Open to God: A Conversation with Pope Francis* (New York: HarperOne, 2013).

4. Karl Rahner, *The Dynamic Element in the Church* (New York: Herder, 1964), 84–170; "On the Question of a Formal Existential Ethics," *Theological Investigations*, vol. 2 (New York: Seabury, 1963), 217–34.

5. Pope John XXIII, Apostolic Constitution for the Convocation of the Second Vatican Council, *Humanae salutis* (1961); the encyclicals *Mater et magistra* (1961) and *Pacem in terris* (1963); *Gaudium et spes* 4, 10–11, 22, among others. Theologically grounded by Marie-Dominique Chenu, "Les signes des temps" in *L'Église dans le monde de ce temps: Constitution Pastorale "Gaudium et Spes,"* ed. Yves Congar and M. Peuchmaurd (Paris: Spes, 1967), 2:205–25.

6. A summary in Walter Kasper, *Katholische Kirche: Wesen-Wirklichkeit-Sendung* (Freiburg i. Br.: Herder, 2011), 452–54 and 567, nn133–35. An English translation is expected in 2015 under the title *The Catholic Church: Nature, Reality, and Mission*.

7. The theory of paradigm shifts derives from Thomas Kuhn's *The Structure of Scientific Revolutions* (Chicago: University of Chicago, 1970). What is meant by a paradigm shift is a change in the parameters and perspective of a theory, which does not annul the content of the earlier theory, but places it in a larger context. Of course, this theory, which has been derived from the history of the natural sciences, can be applied only analogously to the history of theology.

8. Pope John XXIII, Encyclical *Mater et magistra* (1961), 236.

9. See Gustavo Gutierrez, "Aparecida und die vorrangige Option für die Armen," in *Armut: Die Herausforderung für den Glauben*, ed. Gerhard Ludwig Müller (Munich: Kösel, 2014), 138–45; G. Whelan, "*Evangelii gaudium* come 'Teologia contestuale:'

Aiutare la Chiesa ad 'alzarsi al livello dei suoi tempi,'" in *Evangelii gaudium: Il testo ci interroga. Chiavi di lettura, testimonianze e prospettive*, ed. H. M. Yáñez (Rome: Gregorian University, 2014), 23–38.

10. John Henry Newman, *An Essay on The Development of Christian Doctrine* (New York: Cambridge University, 2010). Cf. also Yves Congar, *True and False Reform in the Church* (Collegeville, MN: Liturgical Press, 2011) and *Tradition and Traditions: An Historical and a Theological Essay* (New York: Macmillan, 1967).

III

1. On this issue, see above all: Daniel Deckers, *Papst Franziskus: Wider die Trägheit des Herzens. Eine Biographie* (Munich: Beck, 2014), 23–52.

2. Jorge Bergoglio, *Dios en la ciudad: Praxis de la pastoral urbana en América latina* (Buenos Aires: San Pablo, 2012). Pope Francis, *Evangelii gaudium*, 71–75; also his address on November 27, 2014 to the International Pastoral Congress on the World's Big Cities.

3. Pablo Sudar, Lucio Gera, et al. eds., *Evangelización, liberación y reconciliación: Hacia la nueva evangelización* (Buenos Aires: Ediciones Facultad de Teología de la UCA, 1988). Juan Carlos Scannone, "La filosofía de la liberación: Caracteristicas, corrientes, etapes," *Stromata* 48 (1982): 3–401. Michael Sievernich, ed., *Impulse der Befreiungstheologie für Europa* (Munich: Kaiser, 1988); Ignacio Ellacuría and Jon Sobrino, eds., *Mysterium Liberationis: Fundamental Concepts of Liberation Theology* (Maryknoll: Orbis, 1993). In its Instruction *Libertatis nuntius* (1984), the magisterium's critique pertains to individual aspects of liberation theology, but not liberation theology as a whole. Above all, with regard to the position of Gustavo Gutierrez, for whom I have personal esteem and whom I have never censored, the criticism in

recent times has been essentially relativized. Cf. Gerhard Ludwig Müller, *Armut: Die Herausforderung für den Glauben* (Munich: Kösel, 2014).

4. The collected works of Lucio Gera: V. Szcuy, et al., eds., *Escritos teológico-pastorales de Lucio Gera*, 2 vols. (Buenos Aires: Agape Libros, 2006–07). Cf. Ricardo Ferrara and Carlos María Galli, eds., *Presente y futuro de la teologia en Argentina: Homenaje a Lucio Gera* (Buenos Aires: Paulinas, 1997); "Evangelisierung und Förderung des Menschen" in *Lateinamerika und die katholische Soziallehre*, ed. Peter Hünermann and Juan Carlos Scannone, 3 vols. (Mainz: Matthias Grünewald,1989), 1:245–99. Cf. Margit Eckholt, "'…bei mir erwächst die Theologie aus der Pastoral:' Lucio Gera—ein 'Lehrer in Theologie' von Papst Franziskus," *Stimmen der Zeit* (March 2014): 157–72.

5. This distinction is mentioned on p. 132 in the volume edited by Ignacio Ellacuría and Jon Sobrino, *Mysterium Liberationis*, which apparently had as a consequence that this direction no longer plays a role in the further course of the presentation.

6. See the interview with Antonio Spadaro in *Civiltà cattolica*. Concerning the philosophy of K. C. F. Krause, see the publication of the Friedrich Ebert Stiftung, *El Krausismo y su influencia en América Latina* (Madrid: Friedrich Ebert, 1989).

7. Extensive comments in Decker's *Papst Franziskus: Wider die Trägheit des Herzens*, 31; 53–65. Vallely's thesis that Jorge Bergoglio/Pope Francis has changed from a reactionary to a revolutionary is, therefore, to be critically challenged. Concerning the behavior of the then provincial Jorge Bergoglio during the military dictatorship, see Nello Scavo, *Bergoglios Liste: Papst Franziskus und die argentinische Militärdiktatur* (Freiburg i. Br.: Herder, 2014).

8. I owe these observations to Peter Hünermann. Eugen Biser also calls attention to these connections: *Glaubensprognose: Orientierung in postsäkularistischer Zeit* (Graz: Syria, 1991), 275, 277.

9. Ezio Bolis, Director of the John XXIII Foundation in Bergamo, has beautifully emphasized that point on the basis of the heretofore often little known or unknown sources: *Solo un "Papa buono"? Spiritualità di Giovanni XXIII* (Milan: Paoline, 2014). In his book, *Johannes XXIII: Leben und Wirken des Konzilspapstes* (Mainz: Matthias Grünewald, 2000), Giuseppe Alberigo has already revealed the characteristics of a gospel style—like the emphasis upon gentleness and mercy—that were also defining for Pope Francis.

10. Jörg Ernesti, *Paul VI: Der vergessene Papst* (Freiburg i. Br.: Herder, 2012); Ulrich Nersinger, *Paul VI: ein Papst im Zeichen des Widerspruchs* (Aachen, 2014); Xenio Toscani, *Paolo VI: Una biografia* (Brescia: Istituto Paolo VI, 2014).

11. *Civiltà cattolica* has published an informative article concerning the pope's library: Antonio Spandaro, "La Biblioteca di Papa Francesco," *Civiltà cattolica* 165 (2014): 489–98. Cf. Also Iso Baumer, "Auf den Spuren von Michel de Certeau," *Stimmen der Zeit* 139 (February 2014): 86–96.

12. Pope Francis, Encyclical *Lumen fidei* (2013), 57.

IV

1. See the article "Evangelium," *Lexikon für Theologie und Kirche*, ed. Walter Kasper et al., 3rd ed., 11 vols. (Freiburg i. Br.: Herder, 1993–2001), 3:1058–633 and in *Religion in Geschichte und Gegenwart*, ed. Hans D. Betz et al., 4th ed., 4 vols. (Tübingen: Mohr Siebeck, 1999–2007), 2:1735–42. Concerning its meaning and the history of its meaning, see Walter Kasper, *Dogma unter dem Wort Gottes* (Mainz: Matthias Grünewald, 1965), 7–24; 71–98; *Das Evangelium Jesu Christi* (Freiburg i. Br.: Herder, 2009), 254–72.

2. Thomas Aquinas, *Summa theologiae* II/II q.35; Josef Pieper, *Leisure, the Basis of Culture* (New York: Pantheon, 1952), 73–76; "Acedia" in *Reallexikon für Antike und Christentum*, ed. T.

Klauser, vol. 1 (Stuttgart: Hiersemann, 1950) 62–63; *Lexikon für Theologie und Kirche*, 1:109–10.

3. Friedrich Nietzsche, *Thus Spoke Zarathustra*, in *The Portable Nietzsche*, ed. and trans. Walter Kauffman (New York: Penguin, 1954), prologue 5, p. 129. Cf. Søren Kierkegaard, *The Concept of Anxiety* (Princeton: Princeton University, 1980); *The Sickness Unto Death* (London: Penguin, 2008); Romano Guardini, "Vom Sinn der Schwermut," in *Unterscheidung des Christlichen* (Mainz: Matthias Grünewald, 1963); Martin Heidegger, *Being and Time* (New York: Harper, 1962), Jean Paul Sartre, *Nausea* (New York: New Directions, 1964).

4. Paul Wilhelm von Keppler, *More Joy* (St. Louis: Herder, 1914).

5. Thomas Aquinas, *Summa theologiae* II/II q. 28, a. 1 c.a.

6. See the introduction to the first rule, which was not confirmed as the final rule and testament of St. Francis. Cf. *Die Schriften des hl. Franziskus von Assisi*, ed. Kajetan Esser and Lothar Hardick (Werl: Dietrich Coelde, 1972), 51, 80, 95.

7. Thomas Aquinas, *Summa theologiae* I/II q. 106 a. 1 and 2. Concerning the background of the evangelical movement at that time, see Marie-Dominique Chenu, *Das Werk des hl. Thomas von Aquin*, 2nd ed. (Graz: Styria, 1982), 39–46.

8. *Luther's Works*, 53 vols. (St. Louis: Concordia, 1957–1972); vol. 30, *Catholic Epistles*, ed. Jaroslav Pelikan (St. Louis: Concordia, 1967), 3. Similarly by John Calvin, *The Institutes of the Christian Religion*, 2 vols. (Philadelphia: Westminster, 1977), 1:424–25. Cf. Otto Hermann Pesch, *Theologie der Rechtfertigung bei Martin Luther und Thomas von Aquin: Versuch eines systematisch-theologischen Dialogs* (Mainz: Matthias Grünewald, 1967).

9. Heinrich Denzinger, *Enchiridion symbolorum definitionum et declarationum de rebus fidei et morum*, ed. Peter Hünermann, 44th ed. (Freiburg i. Br.: Herder, 2014), 1501.

10. *Conciliorum oecumenicorum decreta*, ed. Giuseppe Alberigo (Bologna: Istituto per le scienze religiose, 1973), 643–46.

11. See Bolis, *Solo un "Papa buono"? Spiritualità di Giovanni XXIII* (Milan: Paoline, 2014), 27–29.

12. *Enchiridion della nuova evangelizzazione: Testi del Magistero pontificio e conciliare 1939–2012*, ed. Pontifical Council for Promoting the New Evangelization (Vatican City: Libreria Editrice Vaticana, 2012).

13. Philip Jenkins, *The Next Christendom: The Coming of Global Christianity* (New York: Oxford University, 2011); John L. Allen, *The Future Church: How Ten Trends Are Revolutionizing the Catholic Church* (New York: Image Books, 2009); George Weigel, *Evangelical Catholicism: Deep Reform in the 21st Century Church* (New York: Basic Books, 2013).

14. See Adolf von Harnack, *What Is Christianity?* (Philadelphia: Fortress, 1986). Significantly, the original German text, *Das Wesen des Christentums*, was published precisely in 1900.

15. See Kasper, *Dogma unter dem Wort Gottes*, 71–80.

16. Cf. Ulrich Valeske, *Hierarchia veritatum* (Munich: Claudius, 1968); Yves Congar, "The 'Hierarchy of Truths,'" in *Diversity and Communion* (Mystic, CT: Twenty-Third, 1985), 126–33.

17. Thomas Aquinas, *Summa theologiae* II/II q. 1 a 6.

18. Concerning the teaching of Thomas Aquinas about implicit faith (*fides implicita*), see the excursus in the German edition of Thomas's works: *Die deutsche Thomas-Ausgabe* (Salzburg: Pustet, 1950) 15:431–37.

19. Thomas Aquinas, *Summa theologiae* I/II q. 66 a. 4–6; quoted in *Evangelii gaudium*, 37.

20. Luther's preface to the Letter of St. James in *Martin Luther: Selections from His Writings*, ed. John Dillenberger (Garden City, NY: Anchor Books, 1961), 35–36. Out of this, the doctrine of fundamental beliefs developed later in Lutheran and Reformed

orthodoxy. See "Fundamentalartikel" in *Theologische Realenzyklopädie*, ed. Gerhard Müller, Horst Balz, and Gerhard Krause, 36 vols. (Berlin: De Gruyter, 1976–2004), 11:712–38; *Lexikon für Theologie und Kirche*, 4:223; and *Religion in Geschichte und Gegenwart*, 2:412–14. Similarly the Chicago-Lambeth Quadrilateral (1888) in Anglicanism.

21. Well emphasized by H. M. Yáñez, "Tracce di lettura dell'Evangelii gaudium," in *Evangelii gaudium: Il testo ci interroga. Chiavi di lettura, testimonianze e prospettive*, ed. H. M. Yáñez (Rome: Gregorian University, 2014), 9–20.

V

1. Pope Francis, *"Und jetzt beginnen wir diesen Weg": Die ersten Botschaften des Pontifikats* (Freiburg i. Br.: Herder, 2013), 35–38 and more often.

2. Christoph von Schönborn, *We Have Found Mercy: The Mystery of Divine Mercy* (San Francisco: Ignatius Press, 2012). Edith Olk, *Die Barmherzigkeit Gottes als zentrale Quelle des christlichen Lebens* (St. Ottilien: EOS, 2011); Walter Kasper, *Mercy: The Essence of the Gospel and the Key to Christian Life* (New York / Mahwah, NJ: Paulist Press, 2014).

3. Thomas Aquinas, *Summa theologiae* I, q. 21 a. 3 f; q. 25 a. 3 ad 3.

4. Yves Congar, "La miséricorde: Attribut souverain de Dieu," *Vie spirituelle* 106 (1962): 380–95.

5. Thomas Aquinas, *Summa theologiae* I/II q. 107 a. 4.

6. Pope John XXIII, *Journal of a Soul*, trans. Dorothy White (Garden City, NY: Image Books, 1980), 258.

7. See Hans Buob, *Die Barmherzigkeit Gottes und der Menschen: Heilmittel für Seele und Leib nach dem Tagebuch der Schwester Faustyna* (Fremdingen: UNIO, 2000).

8. See Dietrich Bonhoeffer, "Costly Grace," in *The Cost of Discipleship*, trans. R. H. Fuller, rev. ed. (New York: Macmillan, 1972), 35–47. Kasper, *Mercy*, 145–48.

9. See Kasper, *Mercy*, 84–88; bibliography on 230, n12.

10. Kasper, *Mercy*, 131–45.

VI

1. Avery Dulles, *Models of the Church* (Garden City, NY: Doubleday, 1974).

2. Yves Congar has emphasized that point with a lot of historical evidence: "The Church: The People of God" in *Concilium* (1965): 7–19; "'Ecclesia et populus (fidelis)' dans l'ecclésiologie de Saint Thomas," in *Église et Papauté* (Paris: Cerf, 2002), 211–227.

3. Walter Kasper, *Katholische Kirche: Wesen-Wirklichkeit-Sendung* (Freiburg i. Br.: Herder, 2011), 180–87.

4. Concerning this, see ibid., 181.

5. Juan Carlos Scannone, "La teologia di Francesco," *Il Regno* 58 (2013): 128; Scannone, *La Teologia argentina del Pueblo y la Pastoral di Papa Francisco* (2014); J. Xavier, "Spalancando il dinamismo ecclesiale: L'identità ritrovata," in *Evangelii gaudium: Il testo ci interroga. Chiavi di lettura, testimonianze e prospettive*, ed. H. M. Yáñez (Rome: Gregorian University, 2014), 39–52; D. Vitale, "Una chiesa di popolo: Il sensus fidei come principio dell'evangelizzazione," ibid., 53–66; Pope Francis, *La chiesa della misericordia*, ed. Giuliano Vigini (Vatican City: Libreria Editrice Vaticana, 2014).

6. Pope John XXIII, Encyclical *Pacem in terris* (1963), 22; cf. *Gaudium et spes*, 9.

7. *Evangelii gaudium*, 103, quoting the *Compendium of the Social Doctrine of the Church*, published by the Pontifical Council for Justice and Peace (2004).

8. For this position, the pope appeals to John Paul II's Postsynodal Apostolic Exhortation *Christifideles laici* (1988), 51 and the Declaration *Inter insigniores* (1976) from the Congregation for the Doctrine of the Faith.

9. John Henry Newman, "On Consulting the Faithful in Matters of Doctrine" (1859), German translation in *Ausgewählte Werke*, vol. 4 (Mainz: Matthias Grünewald, 1959), 255–92.

10. Peter Hünermann, "Sensus fidei," *Lexikon für Theologie und Kirche*, ed. Walter Kasper et al., 3rd ed., 11 vols. (Freiburg i. Br.: Herder, 1993–2001), 9:465–67.

11. Thus, Xavier, "Spalancando il dinamismo ecclesiale," 50–51. Concerning the problem in general, G. Bonfrate, "La porta aperta dei sacramenti," in Yáñez, *Evangelii gaudium: Il testo ci interroga*, 81–93.

12. See Walter Kasper, *The Gospel of the Family* (New York / Mahwah, NJ: Paulist Press, 2014), 3, 43–47, 52–53.

13. Concerning the theological understanding of truth, Kasper, *Dogma unter dem Wort Gottes* (Mainz: Matthias Grünewald, 1965); "Die Kirche als Ort der Wahrheit," in *Theologie im Diskurs* (Freiburg i. Br.: Herder, 2014), 72–91; "Das Wahrheitsverständnis der Theologie," ibid., 92–120; *Katholische Kirche*, 30–36; 39–41; 373–379.

14. From the abundance of literature, reference is made only to the two exegetical contributions of D. Markl and Th. Söding, which differ in their manner of argumentation, but fundamentally agree in their candor. See their articles in *Zwischen Jesu Wort und Norm: Kirchliches Handeln angesichts von Scheidung und Wiederheirat*, ed. Markus Graulich and Martin Seidnader (Freiburg i. Br.: Herder, 2014).

15. Pope Francis, *"Und jetzt beginnen wir diesen Weg": Die ersten Botschaften des Pontifikats* (Freiburg i. Br.: Herder, 2013), 122–24.

16. "Geduld," *Lexikon für Theologie und Kirche*, 4:339–40; "Oikonomie," ibid., 7:1014–16; "Paideia," ibid., 1272–73.

17. See chapter 2 above, n4; chapter 5 (Model of the spirituality of the Second Vatican Council).

18. Johann Baptist Metz, *Mystik der offenen Augen: Wenn Spiritualität aufbricht* (Freiburg i. Br.: Herder, 2011). Similarly, Tomás Halík, *Berühre die Wunden: Über Leid, Vertrauen und die Kunst der Verwandlung* (Freiburg i. Br.: Herder, 2014).

19. Gisbert Greshake has recently impressed upon us the indispensability of Mariology for ecclesiology in his latest work: *Maria-Ecclesia: Perspektiven einer marianisch grundierten Theologie und Kirchenpraxis* (Regensburg: Friedrich Pustet, 2014).

20. The motif of gentleness and tenderness is also found in other passages: *Evangelii gaudium*, 270, 274, 279, 286.

VII

1. Concerning this, see ch. 1, n8 above.

2. Ignatius of Antioch, "Letter to the Romans," prefatory greeting. See ch. 1, n8 above.

3. Henri de Lubac, *The Splendor of the Church* (New York: Sheed and Ward, 1956). Concerning *communio* ecclesiology, see Walter Kasper, *Katholische Kirche: Wesen-Wirklichkeit-Sendung* (Freiburg i. Br.: Herder, 2011), 45–48, 122–29, 225–38.

4. Congregation for the Doctrine of the Faith, "Some Aspects of the Church Understood as *Communio*" (1992), 9. Cf. Kasper, *Katholische Kirche*, 387–92.

5. Pope John Paul II, Encyclical *Ut unum sint* (1995), 95. Pope Benedict XVI, Address in the Patriarchal Church of Saint George in the Phanar (Istanbul, Turkey) on November 30, 2006. Pope Francis as well appears to pick up the concern of Archbishop John R. Quinn: *The Reform of the Papacy: The Costly Call to Christian Unity* (New York: Crossroad, 1999). Cf. Karl Rahner and Peter

Hünermann, *Die Reform des Papsttums* (Freiburg i. Br.: Herder, 2001).

6. Cf. Kasper, *Katholische Kirche*, 382–87.

7. See the interview of Pope Francis with Spadaro in *Civiltà cattolica* 164 (2013): 466

8. Irenaeus of Lyon, *Against Heresies*, IV, 26, 2.

9. Even this idea is not entirely new. Max Seckler has demonstrated its presence already in the father of modern theological methodology, Melchior Cano. See his article "Die ekklesiologische Bedeutung des Systems der 'loci theologici': Erkenntnistheoretische Katholizität und strukturale Weisheit," in *Die schiefen Wände des Lehrhauses: Katholizität als Herausforderung* (Freiburg i. Br.: Herder, 1988), 79–104.

10. Johann Adam Möhler, *Unity in the Church or the Principle of Catholicism*, ed. and trans. Peter C. Erb (Washington, DC: Catholic University of America, 1996), 262.

VIII

1. Pope Francis, *"Und jetzt beginnen wir diesen Weg": Die ersten Botschaften des Pontifikats* (Freiburg i. Br.: Herder, 2013), 47–50. Riccardo Burigana, *Un cuore solo: Papa Francesco e l'unità della Chiesa* (Milan: Edizioni Terra Santa, 2014). Cf. Walter Kasper, "Die ökumenische Vision von Papst Franziskus," in *Wege zur Erneuerung des Glaubens*, Festschrift for Kurt Cardinal Koch, ed. George Augustin and M. Schulze (Freiburg i. Br.: Herder, 2015).

2. For a detailed description of the situation, Walter Kasper, "Vorwort: Einheit—damit die Welt glaubt," in *Wege zur Einheit der Christen: Schriften zur Ökumene 1* (Freiburg i. Br.: Herder, 2012), 17–34.

3. Pope Hadrian VI already expressed shared responsibility for the Reformation at the Diet of Nuremberg in 1522; Pope Paul VI asked for pardon already at the opening of the second session

of the Second Vatican Council. Concerning Pope John Paul II's words and gestures of reconciliation, see the document from the International Theological Commission: "Memory and Reconciliation: The Church and the Faults of the Past" (1999).

4. Jorge Mario Bergoglio and Abraham Skorka, *On Heaven and Earth*, trans. Alejandro Bermudez and Howard Goodman (New York: Image Books, 2013), 220.

5. Ibid., 217, concerning Oscar Cullmann's *Unity through Diversity: Its Foundation and a Contribution to the Discussion concerning the Possibilities of Its Actualization* (Minneapolis: Fortress, 1988). On this matter, Joseph Ratzinger, *Zum Fortgang der Ökumene* (Freiburg i. Br.: Herder, 2010), 734–36.

6. Kasper, *Wege zur Einheit*, 222–33; 361–64 (in reference to Johann Sebastian Drey und Johann Adam Möhler).

7. Harding Meyer, *Versöhnte Verschiedenheit: Aufsätze zur ökumenischen Theologie*, vol. 1 (Frankfurt a.M.: Lembeck, 1998), 101–19.

8. Document of the Joint Commission for Theological Dialogue between the Roman Catholic Church and the Orthodox Church, "The Mystery of the Church and of the Eucharist in the Light of the Mystery of the Holy Trinity," chapter 3, sections 1–4, available at http://www.vatican.va/roman_curia/pontifical_coun cils/chrstuni/ch_orthodox_docs/rc_pc_chrstuni_doc_19820706_ munich_en.html.

9. In *Evangelii gaudium*, the image of the polyhedron is only described in general terms, but at the meeting with a Pentecostal community in Caserta on July 28, 2014, it is used as a description of ecumenical unity.

10. John Paul II, Encyclical *Ut unm sint* (1995); Ecumenical Commemoration of the Witnesses to the Faith in the Twentieth Century, May 7, 2000; Apostolic Letter, *Novo millennio ineunte* (2001), 7.

11. Tertullian, *Apologeticum* 50, 13. Cf. Walter Kasper, *Ökumene der Märtyrer: Theologie und Spiritualität des Martyriums* (Edition Schönblick: Books on Demand, 2013).

IX

1. Extensive contributions to these themes in *Evangelii gaudium: Il testo ci interroga. Chiavi di lettura, testimonianze e prospettive*, ed. H. M. Yáñez (Rome: Gregorian University, 2014).

2. Reference is to be made to the Council's Declaration on the Relation of the Church to Non-Christian Religions, *Nostra Aetate*; and to the pertinent chapters of the pastoral constitution, *Gaudium et spes*, 40–45, 53–62. Cf. also the writings of the International Theological Commission: *Christianity and the World Religions* (1997); *God the Trinity and the Unity of Humanity: Christian Monotheism and Its Opposition to Violence* (2014).

3. Pope Francis, *"Und jetzt beginnen wir diesen Weg": Die ersten Botschaften des Pontifikats* (Freiburg i. Br.: Herder, 2013), 51–52.

4. Message for the World Day of Peace, 2014.

5. Concerning Jewish-Christian dialogue: Jorge Mario Bergoglio and Abraham Skorka, *On Heaven and Earth*, trans. Alejandro Bermudez and Howard Goodman (New York: Image Books, 2013); Address to the Members of the International Jewish Committee on Interreligious Consultations on June 24, 2013.

6. Meeting with the bishops of Asia on August 17, 2014.

7. Homily for the beatification of Paul Yun Ji-Chung and 123 companions on August 16, 2014.

X

1. Pope Francis, *"Und jetzt beginnen wir diesen Weg": Die ersten Botschaften des Pontifikats* (Freiburg i. Br.: Herder, 2013), 31.

Similar comments in his address to the diplomatic corps, ibid., 54–55; *Evangelii gaudium*, 198.

2. The texts are collected in Thomas Laubach and Stefanie Wahl, eds., *Arme Kirche? Die Botschaft des Papstes in der Diskussion*, (Freiburg i. Br.: Herder, 2014), 13–34; A. Buckenmaier and L. Weimer, eds., *A Poor People for the Poor in the World? The Challenge of Pope Francis* (Vatican City, 2014).

3. J. Alt, "Eine arme Kirche für die Armen," *Stimmen der Zeit* 139 (2014): 361–62; Laubach and Wahl, *Arme Kirche?*, 49–54; H. M. Yáñez, "L'opzione preferenziale per i poveri," in *Evangelii gaudium: Il testo ci interroga. Chiavi di lettura, testimonianze e prospettive*, ed. H. M. Yáñez (Rome: Gregorian University, 2014), 249–60.

4. Gustavo Gutierrez has already emphasized that clearly: "Aparecida und die vorrangige Option für die Armen," in *Armut: Die Herausforderung für den Glauben*, ed. Gerhard Ludwig Müller (Munich: Kösel, 2014), 144–66. Cf. the thorough analysis of the texts from Pope Francis in Laubach and Wahl, *Arme Kirche?*, 37–45.

5. Marie-Dominique Chenu, "Vatican II and the Church of the Poor," *Concilium* (1977/4): 56–61.

6. The German text of the Catacomb Pact can be found in *Concilium* (D) 13 (1977): 262–63. An English translation can be found in the *National Catholic Reporter*'s commemoration of the hundredth anniversary of the birth of Bishop Helder Camara: http://ncronline.org/news/peace-justice/urgent-need-return-being-church-poor. See also Th. Fornet-Ponse, "Für eine arme Kirche: Der Katakombenpakt von 1965 als Beispiel der Entweltlichung," *Stimmen der Zeit* 230 (2012): 651–61; Luigi Bettazzi, *Das Zweite Vatikanische Konzil: Neustart der Kirche aus den Wurzeln des Glaubens* (Würzburg: Echter Verlag, 2012).

7. Roberto Morozzo della Rocca, ed., *Oscar Romero: Un vescovo centroamericano tra guerra fredda e rivoluzione* (Milan: Cinisello Balsamo, 2003).

8. *Concluding Document: Aparecida, 13 a 31 de Mayo de 2007* (Bogotá: Consejo Episcopal Latinoamericano, 2008), 8.3.

9. *Evangelii gaudium*, 25, 83, 122, 124.

10. Pope John Paul II, Encyclical *Sollicitudo rei socialis* (1987) 42; Encyclical *Centesimus annus* (1991) 57; Apostolic Letter *Tertio millennio adveniente* (1994) 51; Apostolic Letter *Novo millennio ineunte* (2001), 49. Pope Benedict in his opening address in Aparecida on May 13, 2007. Cf. "Option für die Armen," *Lexikon für Theologie und Kirche*, ed. Walter Kasper et al., 3rd ed., 11 vols. (Freiburg i. Br.: Herder, 1993–2001), 6:1078.

11. Jürgen Erbacher, *Entweltlichung der Kirche?* (Freiburg i. Br.: Herder, 2012).

12. Karl Rahner, "The Theology of Poverty," in *Theological Investigations*, vol. 8 (New York: Herder, 1971), 168–214.

13. Dietrich Bonhoeffer, *Letters and Papers from Prison*, ed. Eberhard Bethge (New York: Macmillan, 1966), 239–40. Similar thoughts in Alfred Delp, *Prison Meditations of Father Alfred Delp* (New York: Herder, 1963), 114–15.

14. *Gemeinsame Synode der Bistümer in der Bundesrepublik Deutschland* (Freiburg i. Br.: Herder, 1976), 105; 109–10. Cf. Johann Baptist Metz, *Zeit der Orden: Zur Mystik und Politik der Nachfolge* (Freiburg i. Br.: Herder, 1977), 48–63; Metz, *Gottespassion: Zur Ordensexistenz heute* (Freiburg i. Br.: Herder, 1991), 25–30.

15. Karl Rahner, "The Unreadiness of the Church's Members to Accept Poverty," in *Theological Investigations*, vol. 14 (New York: Crossroad Book, 1976), 270–79. From a French perspective, Yves Congar, *Power and Poverty in the Church* (London: Chapman, 1965); Congar, "The Place of Poverty in Christian Life in an Affluent Society," *Concilium* 15 (1966): 28–39.

16. Th. Schmidt, "Kirche im Auf-Bruch," in Laubach and Wahl, *Arme Kirche?* 143–51.

XI

1. *Lateinamerika und die katholische Soziallehre*, ed. Peter Hünermann and Juan Carlos Scannone, 3 vols. (Mainz: Matthias Grünewald, 1989). More recent articles from S. Bernal, D. Alonso-Lasheras, and H. M. Yáñez in *Evangelii gaudium: Il testo ci interroga. Chiavi di lettura, testimonianze e prospettive*, ed. H. M. Yáñez (Rome: Gregorian University, 2014). I. Pies offers a differentiated view: "Papst Franziskus – kein Gegner des Marktes: Eine wirtschaftsethische Stellungnahme zu 'Evangelii gaudium,'" *Stimmen der Zeit* 139 (214): 233–42.

2. Thomas Laubach and Stefanie Wahl, eds., *Arme Kirche? Die Botschaft des Papstes in der Diskussion*, (Freiburg i. Br.: Herder, 2014), 36. The quotations from the German media are augmented by D. Alonso-Lasheras with others from the international press. See his article in Yáñez, *Evangelii gaudium: Il testo ci interroga*.

3. Derisively people have also spoken of a theory of horse droppings: one only has to give a horse enough oats, then a lot falls to the ground and the sparrows have something to pick up.

4. Ronald Reagan (1911–2004), president of the United States from 1981 to 1989.

5. *Evangelii gaudium*, 62, 145, 178, 182, 184, 190, 196, 198, 219, 221.

6. Pontifical Council for Justice and Peace, *Compendium of the Social Doctrine of the Church*; *Evangelii gaudium* 182–83, 190, 221, 240.

7. Concerning work as the key to social questions, see John Paul II, *Laborem exercens* (1981).

8. "Gastfreundschaft," *Lexikon für Theologie und Kirche*, ed. Walter Kasper et al., 3rd ed., 11 vols. (Freiburg i. Br.: Herder, 1993–2001), 4:299–301.

9. Pope Pius XII, Apostolic Constitution *Exul familia* (1952); Pope John XXIII, Encyclical *Pacem in terris* (1963), 12; 57; Pope Paul VI, Apostolic Letter *Octogesima adveniens* (1971), 17.

10. R. M. Micallef, "Il ritorno del linguaggio profetico sul tema dell'immigrazione," in Yáñez, *Evangelii gaudium: Il testo ci interroga*, 235–47.

11. Pope John Paul II, Encyclical *Centesimus annus* (1991), 42.

12. Pope Benedict XVI, Encyclical *Caritas in veritate* (2009), 6.

13. Ibid., 2 (quoted in *Evangelii gaudium*, 205). Cf. Walter Kasper, *Mercy: The Essence of the Gospel and the Key to Christian Life* (New York / Mahwah, NJ: Paulist Press, 2014), 189–90.

14. *Evangelii gaudium* 183, 189, 219, 288, among others. At length, for instance, in his speech during a visit to the Food and Agriculture Organization (FAO) on November 20, 2014, as well as in speeches before the European Parliament and the Council of Europe on November 25, 2014.

15. His speech on November 15, 2014 to the Italian Catholic Physicians' Association refutes this charge.

16. P. Xalxo, "Le orme ecologiche della nuova evangelizzazione," in Yáñez, *Evangelii gaudium: Il testo ci interroga*, 261–74.

17. Pope Benedict XVI, Encyclical *Caritas in veritate* (2009), 48; Message for the World Day of Peace, 2010: "If You Want to Cultivate Peace, Protect Creation."

18. Pope Francis, *"Und jetzt beginnen wir diesen Weg": Die ersten Botschaften des Pontifikats* (Freiburg i. Br.: Herder, 2013), 42–46; cf. *Evangelii gaudium*, 215.

19. See Jorge Mario Bergoglio/ Pope Francis, *La bellezza educherà il mondo*, with afterword by Vittorino Andreoli (Bologna: EMI, 2014); Jorge Mario Bergoglio, *Erziehen mit Anspruch und Leidenschaft* (Freiburg i. Br.: Herder, 2014).

XII

1. Theodor Haecker, *Virgil: Father of the West* (New York: Sheed and Ward, 1975); Hans Urs von Balthasar, *The Office of Peter and the Structure of the Church*, 2nd ed. (San Francisco: Ignatius, 2007), 361–81; Jochen Jorendt and Romedio Schmitz-Esser, eds., *Rom—Nabel der Welt: Macht, Glaube, Kultur von der Antike bis heute* (Darmstadt: Wissenschaftliche Buchgesellschaft, 2010).

2. That is true already of Pope Pius XII. Cf. Pope Paul VI, Apostolic Letter *Pacis nuntius* (1964), with which he proclaimed the founder of monastic life, Benedict of Nursia, the patron of all of Europe. Cf. Pope John Paul II, especially his Apostolic Exhortation *Ecclesia in Europa* (2003). Pope Benedict XVI has spoken repeatedly about Europe's legacy and its crisis, in which Europe runs the risk of losing its soul. See Clemens Sedmak and Stephan Otto Horn, eds., *Die Seele Europas: Papst Benedikt XVI und die europäische Identität* (Regensburg: Pustet, 2011).

3. Pope Francis' address to the European Parliament in Strasbourg on November 25, 2014.

4. The concept of transcendent dignity must be correctly understood. What is meant is a dignity that is posited and inherent in human beings as human, which they do not give to themselves and that also is not given to them by society, the state, or other party. It is, therefore, inalienable. In principle, it is a secular translation of what the Bible means when it speaks of the human being as being an image of God.

5. Pope Francis' address to the European Parliament.

6. Pope Francis' address to the Council of Europe in Strasbourg on November 25, 2014.

7. Thus in the speech to the International Pastoral Congress on the World's Big Cities, immediately after his return from Strasbourg on November 27, 2014. This secular character ought

not be confused with a secularization that is inimical to religion or the church (nor is it to be confused with the French *laicité*). Secularism acknowledges and respects, together with the Second Vatican Council (GS 36, 41, 56, 76; AA 7) the legitimate autonomy of culture and the state, and with the Declaration on Religious Freedom, *Dignitatis humanae*, it acknowledges and respects a plurality of cultures and religions without relinquishing Christianity's claim to truth. However, secularism derives therefrom—in distinction from secularization—no hostile or indifferent relation, but rather a positively constructive relation of dialogue, collaboration, and mutual enrichment (GS 40; 76).

8. Pope Francis' address to the Council of Europe. The concept of transversality, which derives from mathematics and geology, is found nowadays also in economics (the theory of exchange rates), sociology, political science, and psychology as well as in the aesthetics and theory of modern media. In philosophy the concept of transversality has become fundamental in view of the ineluctable plurality of our globalized world. It stands for a theory of rational communication and creative interaction between different ethnic, cultural, religious, and other kinds of groups. In the process, it seeks to avoid the relativism and the mutual indifference of a postmodern *anything goes* attitude as well as the neocolonial, Eurocentric exclusiveness and one-sided normativity of Western modernity. It has to do with a transmodern concept of reason, which creatively links identity and plurality and thus enables a creative coexistence and cooperation, in which the identity of each respective culture and religion is cherished and, in the encounter with other cultures and religions, is simultaneously enriched. In Latin America, this way of thinking is found above all in Enrique Dussel, who comes from Argentina. Dussel, *Der Gegendiskurs der Moderne: Kölner Vorlesungen* (Vienna: Turia and Kant, 2012). In German-speaking regions, reference is

to be made to Wolfgang Welsch, *Unsere postmoderne Moderne* (Weinheim: VCH, 1987); *Vernunft: Die zeitgenössische Vernunftkritik und das Konzept der transversalen Vernunft* (Frankfurt a. M.: Suhrkamp, 1995).

9. See the historically well-informed studies by Rémi Brague, *Eccentric Culture: A Theory of Western Civilization* (South Bend, IN: St. Augustine's Press, 2002).

10. With Paul VI it was the relation of faith and culture in the encyclical *Ecclesiam suam* (1964) and in the Apostolic Exhortation *Evangelii nuntiandi* (1975). With John Paul II it was the relation of faith and knowledge in the encyclical *Fides et ratio* (1998), a problem that became absolutely essential for Benedict XVI, especially in his Regensburg lecture on faith and reason on September 12, 2006.

11. Pope Francis' address to the Council of Europe.

12. Ibid.

13. Pope Francis' address to the European Parliament.

OUTLOOK FOR THE FUTURE

1. Andrea Riccardi, *Franziskus: Papst der Überraschungen* (Würzburg: Echter, 2014), 235.

2. Ibid., 241.